AN ILLINOIS SAMPLER

AN ILLINOIS SAMPLER

Teaching and Research
on the Prairie

Edited by Mary-Ann Winkelmes
and Antoinette Burton,
with Kyle Mays

UNIVERSITY OF ILLINOIS PRESS

Urbana, Chicago, and Springfield

Library of Congress Control Number: 2014942436
ISBN 978-0-252-03864-8 (hardcover)
ISBN 978-0-252-08023-4 (paperback)
ISBN 978-0-252-09657-0 (ebook)

CONTENTS

ACKNOWLEDGMENTS

This book, like the collaborative nexus it models, is the work of many hands. We thank Richard Wheeler, former interim provost of the University of Illinois, for supporting our efforts, and the current University of Illinois provost, Ilesanmi Adesida, for sustaining them. Barbara J. Wilson, executive vice provost for faculty and academic affairs, had a key role in endorsing our project, and we are grateful to her as well. A host of people managed logistical and business aspects of this undertaking. Among them, Nikki Hodge in the Office of the Provost and Tom Bedwell in the History Department have been especially gracious and helpful. Bill Regier at the University of Illinois Press has encouraged this project from the start. We appreciate his enthusiasm and the help we have received from his staff at the press, including Laurie Matheson, Vijay Shah, Jennifer Reichlin, and Alice Ennis.

Thanks to a series of lively workshops in 2012–13, each of the contributors had a hand in the crafting of several essays beyond their own and in editing the final version of our introduction as well. The authors' willingness to submit to critique, to make explicit the core values that animate their vision of public higher education, and to offer generous feedback to colleagues has been instrumental to the excitement we feel about both the book and also the ways we hope it will inform conversations about higher education. Kyle Mays's contribution to this project has been nothing short of amazing. Though he began as our assistant, he quickly became our collaborator and friend. His essay, which comes at the very end of the book, speaks to the impact of talking and writing about teaching and research for college and university teachers yet to come.

To the students past, present, and future who inspire us in our role as educators every day, we offer our greatest thanks. This book is dedicated to you.

Antoinette Burton and Mary-Ann Winkelmes
URBANA, ILLINOIS

INTRODUCTION

Charting Common Ground in the Teaching-Research Nexus

Mary-Ann Winkelmes
Antoinette Burton

This unique account of the teaching-research-learning enterprise arrives at an important moment in the evolution of higher education, when concerns about cost and accessibility have driven some to dissect teaching, research, and learning into separately fundable commodities. In this book, leading scholar-educators from across the disciplines at the University of Illinois offer insights into how their vocation integrates teaching, research, and learning in a complex and evolving practice—a collaborative enterprise that connects faculty, students, and the society in promoting the discovery, understanding, and application of new knowledge. All the contributors identify distinctive ways their day-to-day work unites teaching with research and learning toward the goal of improving public life in their institutions, communities, state, country, and across the world. This book is evidence of their aspirations, their commitment to public higher education, and the transformative impact of learning when research and teaching are intimately linked.

Readers may recognize the authors primarily through the lens of their discipline or specialty: as a scientist or an artist, a lab or field researcher, a performer or an inventor. The contributors collected here span disciplines from dance to medicine, from anthropology to engineering, from literature to earth sciences, from mathematics to music. They vary not only by expertise but also in age, gender, nationality, career stage, and even their position in the academic hierarchy. What they all share is an appreciation for how teaching, learning, and research can cohere in practices that advance both the production of new knowledge and the transformation of students into highly capable, engaged citizens ready to take up whatever life and workplace challenges lie ahead of them. Readers of this book cannot help but note how passionately these faculty feel about their research-teaching-learning enterprise, and how creatively they strive to promote it with their students in classrooms and other contexts every day.

This book's varied and powerful articulations of the research-and-teaching feedback loop developed, as Kyle Mays explains in his chapter, from a year's discussions among authors connected more by their conceptions of learning than by their subject matter. Among the most salient findings that emerge from the following chapters are these:

- In a public land-grant university, teaching and research take multiple and sometimes unexpected forms inside and beyond the traditional classroom or laboratory or archive.
- Innovation happens not only in research, but also via active engagement with students, in both planned and unanticipated ways.
- Teaching, research, and learning are experimental practices, where trial-and-error methods drive innovation and require agility and adaptation on the part of both teachers and students.
- Collaboration—across disciplines, institutions, and nations; and among faculty, students, and community partners—is the catalyst for the discoveries, learning, and societal benefits that emerge from the feedback loop between teaching and research.

These themes animate and unite these chapters, which are brimming with insights about the impact of teaching-and-research practices on students, faculty, and communities far beyond the brick-and-mortar campus. For some of this book's teacher-researchers, students can be guides for their efforts to make leading-edge research relevant to the public and important for future generations. Richard Tapping, Carol Spindel, and Nancy Abelmann are engaged in new and successful research that benefits a broad public as a result of their interactions with students in the classroom or laboratory. Tapping's medical students urged him to make more direct links between basic science research and clinical medical practice, which has resulted in his current National Institutes of Health–funded project on autoimmune disease. Spindel's creative-writing students challenged her to follow her own advice about tackling difficult subjects, motivating her to complete a critically acclaimed book and to serve as a national spokesperson—two accomplishments she might never have realized otherwise. As Spindel puts it, "I encourage them to grab hold of their passions and obsessions, no matter how quirky, and write about them. And as I teach, I am learning to do the same." In a similar vein, reactions by students in Abelmann's courses to data about Korean American students provided additional new data that she and they studied together, in a classroom that became a kind of "social science

INTRODUCTION: CHARTING COMMON GROUND xi

research laboratory," generating knowledge and insights with implications for student life, immigration policy, and debates about globalization and higher education.

In history, chemistry, biology, public health, geography, geology, engineering, women's studies, mathematics, and other fields, authors in this volume illuminate a variety of efforts to engage their students in meaningful learning via research as they begin their course of study, so that the excitement of discovery motivates them to learn the discipline's basic (if difficult) tools and principles. The range of such opportunities is, frankly, breathtaking. Flavia Andrade, Lauren Denofrio-Corrales, Yi Lu, Luisa-Maria Rosu, Jayadev Athreya, Thomas Bassett, Bruce Fouke, Mark Steinberg, and Karen Flynn want to replicate the thrill of learning through discovery for their students, and work to integrate research-based learning into the Illinois undergraduate curriculum. Flynn does so through a montage of multimedia and multilingual sources, encouraging students to think about how Baby Cham and Alicia Keys's music video "Ghetto Story" illuminates black women's lives across broad transnational spaces. In Andrade's health statistics courses, students learn the tools of statistical analysis by sharing and studying data about their own eating habits, exercise, and social interactions—discoveries that help them appreciate in concrete ways just exactly how numbers and data impact their daily lives and well-being. Denofrio-Corrales, Lu, and Rosu help first-semester science students begin cross-disciplinary biochemistry or engineering research projects as members of laboratory research teams, motivated by questions as simple as "when egg whites harden in the pan, why do they change from a transparent goop to a white solid?" and problems as complex as designing a mechanical system that can provide prescription pills remotely to patients. Athreya's students playfully engage mathematical principles. They come to appreciate, as he does, that math is not a "stately march" to the mountaintops of calculus or algebra but an aesthetic experience, like "painting with numbers." Bassett's geography students learn about the global cotton trade by analyzing the origins of their own T-shirts. In the process, they develop a greater understanding of the meaning of subsidies for West African cotton farmers—while he becomes drawn into new research directions through their questions and discoveries. Fouke's students swim in coral reefs and record primary research observations in waterproof notebooks. Steinberg's students leaf through past and contemporary print and online media to learn about making history by analyzing primary sources. Even seasoned historians such as Steinberg can find their work startling: as he notes, "what has surprised me, but I have come to value, is how students insist on seeing connections to their own lives, to our own times, and how this helps them see the past in fresh ways."

In today's world, the rapid evolution of knowledge in emerging disciplines requires teachers, students, and other collaborators to learn, research, and teach together as a regular class activity. In this context, many of the authors see their classrooms as sites for making sense of evolving, new knowledge at the forefront of their disciplines. Academic fields like artistic design, computer programming, landscape architecture, dance, and library and information science are developing new insights by crossing traditional subject area borders and by seamlessly blending real-world practice, teaching, research, and learning. Bradley Tober, William Sullivan, Rebecca Nettl-Fiol, and Kate Williams are among the educators who work alongside their students while guiding them in how to understand and benefit from an abundance of new discoveries. Tober helps art students make sense of and contribute to the evolving principles of coding (i.e., software programming) that are remaking the frameworks of design practice, while Sullivan challenges his students and himself to integrate new environmental research into city planning through a focus on what he calls "the Latest Story" in that area of inquiry. Nettl-Fiol collaborates with students and professors alike from around the globe as they research and teach each other new ways of embedding principles from body-mind disciplines and developmental movement concepts into contemporary dance practices. Williams guides her library students as she and they together explore how communities share information in cyberspace, at the same time that they are doing the work of librarians serving the public using the library's computers. For these professors, teaching *is* both collaborative research and contemporary practice.

The teaching-and-research work represented in this book circles the globe, connecting and benefiting teachers and students in environments and communities beyond the classroom in real and virtual spaces worldwide. D. Fairchild Ruggles and her colleagues encourage incarcerated men to develop critical thinking skills, in an environment that "many would consider actively hostile to the human spirit" but one in which intellectual engagement and excitement take root. Julie Gunn and her collaborators engage audiences in concert halls worldwide. Flynn and Abelmann involve Black and Korean diasporic communities of professionals and students in their research and teaching. Bassett helps his students understand their distant yet significant connections with West African farmers. Williams and her local and distant students serve public library users in Champaign-Urbana, nationwide, and in China, creating a whole new class of educated users whom she calls

"Cybernavigators"—with all the promise of discovery and innovation the name entails.

For practitioners such as Gunn and Fouke, good research requires more than making breakthrough discoveries. It necessitates making those findings understood and useful to a global public audience. Gunn's discoveries about musical collaboration and performance matter most when the research takes life in a performance that changes an audience's perception of the music. "Collaboration in small groups is how we learn to speak for ourselves and listen to others (at the same time!) and to find common ground," she writes. "And that sort of collaboration is a microcosm of a larger kind: the collaboration between the creators of art, the performers, and the audience." Fouke's conception of a good scientist requires sharing new discoveries that become relevant only when the general public understands those discoveries as indispensable to big, even planetary questions, such as how life arose on earth and how we can develop new forms of genuinely sustainable energy. His goal is nothing less than to train the student to become "a citizen scientist of the world."

At a historical moment when there is much talk of the obsolescence of traditional college campuses and classrooms, and of the efficacy of MOOCs (massive open online courses) for a new global workforce, the authors represented in this book make an implicit and explicit case that teaching and research must work as one to produce the combination of diverse *and* unified learning experiences that inspire students, benefit the public, and help us meet the millennial challenges we all face. By now, most faculty in brick-and-mortar classrooms make use of technology in class meetings, discussions, and hands-on activities to such an extent that even a relatively traditional lecture on the Grimm brothers' literature by Laurie Johnson has become a hypermedial experience. More significantly, what emerges from this volume is an awareness of the wide variety of learning spaces that are available to students at the University of Illinois: from virtual to concrete, from desks to drafting tables to laboratory benches to archive shelves, from the dance floor to the ocean floor, the prairies to the mountaintops. Illinois students have the opportunity to occupy different kinds of experimental sites where they both witness and help to shape the kinds of innovation and discovery that an integrated research-and-teaching practice routinely delivers, for the benefit of local communities, state residents, and fellow citizens around the world.

This book's varied and powerful examples of the research-and-teaching feedback loop share a conviction about the capacity of research and teaching, together, to inspire students and to transform the world we live in. Such a conviction has arguably never been as important as at this particular moment, when we are inundated by data and overwhelmed by the scale and complexity that contemporary problems—from global climate change to economic catastrophe to endemic violence to political crisis—pose to our collective futures. As Williams so wisely writes in her essay, "when what you are studying is changing rapidly, teaching has to stick close to the latest research." The public land-grant university, driven by its tremendous teaching-and-research engine, models both a comprehensive approach to the challenges of the day and a vision of integrated solutions. As we hope *An Illinois Sampler* shows, teachers and students, learning and research, are, together, the beating heart of the ambitious, ever-evolving project of higher education.

A Sense of the Earth

Bruce W. Fouke
Departments of Geology and Microbiology
Institute for Genomic Biology

How did Life arise on Earth and is it elsewhere in the universe? What is the next source of sustainable energy? Will the emergence of infectious disease accompany global climate change? These are but a small sampling of the immensely challenging and complex scientific questions facing our society. However, no single branch of scientific research can provide meaningful answers. Earth scientists are therefore developing the new discipline of Systems Geobiology, which links multi-scale geological, biological, physical, and chemical processes. This systems geobiology emphasis necessitates the broad cross-disciplinary integration of reductionist and holistic approaches, integrated field and laboratory experimentation, and synthesis across broad spatial and temporal scales.

One of my objectives as a geoscience educator is to nurture a sense of the Earth in young natural scientists by regularly bringing them into the field. The field environment is the only educational setting where students witness firsthand the complexity and immensity of natural processes while simultaneously facing core human uncertainty regarding wilderness and the unknown. As a result, there is no substitute for educational experiences in the field, which uniquely meld science and humanity to provide the type of holistic integration needed to approach the most vexing issues facing our society. This is especially true for the earth sciences, where the goal is to reawaken the intimate primordial connection that all human beings have with their home planet. Yet because few have maintained the basic curiosity and inquisitiveness they had as children, many adults no longer seek to understand their own personal existence in the context of the historical evolution and modern-day composition of the Earth.

A cornerstone of effective field-based systems geobiology education is to emphasize that scientific endeavor is a distinctly human experience. This recognizes the power and importance of human observation, thought and emotional engagement during the ongoing scientific process of data collection and synthesis. From my perspective, this is also what makes science a populist endeavor (*citizen scientists*) rather than an activity available to only a few select people. Application of all the human senses and intellectual faculties, coupled with both the will and opportunity to learn about and understand one's surroundings, means that the capacity to conduct science is widely disseminated within our society. This is the fundamental transformation required for someone to become a citizen scientist of the world. Paramount among these capacities is the power of human observation and the need to return time and again to a complex natural system to simply observe and continually test previous ideas about how a natural system works. The formal progression along this field-based learning pathway begins with presentation of the age-old adage that "analogy identifies anomaly." In other words, the unknown (the anomaly) is identified as worthy of study and investigated via direct comparison to what the observer has previously known (the analogy). The most alluring and enthralling of natural environments are generally those that are the most different from what we have previously experienced in our lives. The unique size, shape, and color of natural wonders such as the Grand Canyon or Old Faithful make them irresistibly fascinating expressly because they are so foreign to our everyday experience.

The challenge lies in how to structure and deliver rigorous and memorable educational content while teaching systems geobiology in a wide variety of natural field environments. Obviously, no perfect solution exists for how to teach effectively in the field, the classroom, or the laboratory. Effective instruction is further complicated in higher education settings by the irony that the vast majority of university faculty members in the natural sciences have never received formal education in how to teach. Yet, intuition and commitment allow us to persist, and trial-and-error experimentation during my own twenty-five years of global field instruction has distilled the basic suite of teaching approaches presented in this chapter. These have proven to consistently and dramatically enrich the field-based learning experience of students of diverse backgrounds and nationalities in breathtaking natural environments around the world.

A further challenge for students is that real scientific inquiry does not follow the traditional scientific method—often first taught in middle school as a recipe-like mechanical series of events. In reality, when conducted rigorously and reproducibly, science generates as many new questions as it answers, a process I call scientific inquiry (figure 1). Stage 1 of scientific inquiry is initiation, where relevant and meaningful scientific questions are chosen

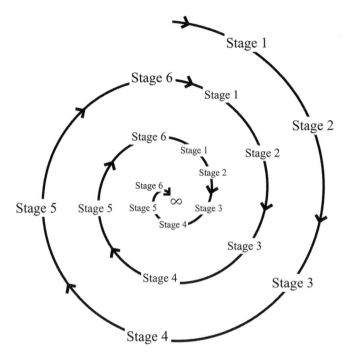

FIGURE 1. The process of scientific inquiry, in which six progressive stages are reiterated during scientific endeavor.

and developed through the use of observation, intuition, knowledge from previous work (i.e., published studies and personal communications), personal observations, and thought experiments. Stage 2 is preexperimentation, where results from stage 1 are reworked into initial working hypotheses in the following ways: (1) by using logical thought experiments (i.e., dialectical and methodological skepticism approaches); (2) by applying integrated modeling approaches; (3) by making reasonable estimates; (4) by using analogy with known phenomena to identify phenomenological anomalies that are not yet understood; and (5) by being willing either to support or to reject basic conventional thinking. Stage 3 is pilot experimentation, in which pilot study experiments are designed and implemented in the field and in the laboratory. These pilot studies receive feedback from simultaneous theoretical modeling efforts. Once the pilot data from stage 3 have justified the experimental design and proposed hypothesis testing, then full experimentation is completed in stage 4, in which newly produced data are immediately modeled to test the targeted hypotheses. Stage 5 is a postexperimentation phase of thorough synthesis, evaluation, and modeling of the completed experimental data set to interpret interactive geological and biological relationships. And finally, reiteration and reinitiation constitute stage 6 of the scientific inquiry process, wherein scientific inquiry is embarked on anew with refined questions and hypotheses that can be pursued in the next full cycle.

Like researchers, students in the field are immediately confronted by the coupled challenges posed by scale and complexity. So that students can address and incorporate these factors, the primary physical, chemical, and biological components of systems geobiology can be placed into a "Powers of Ten" spatial and temporal framework. For example, most natural environmental systems span a dynamic length-scale spatial range from 10^{-9} to 10^5 m. This illustrates for students that analyses ranging from the single cell to entire ecosystems can be simultaneously measured, correlated, and mechanistically linked with geological processes.

Another remarkably important and helpful tool for students engaged in field-based education and research is the field notebook. The bright cover and thickly woven wood fiber and cotton pages of field notebooks allow them to be submerged in water, lost in forest, dropped in caves, and buried in snow, but eventually retrieved without being destroyed by the elements. Field notebooks can survive virtually every terrestrial or submarine calamity, with the possible exceptions of fire and theft. I encourage students to record their entire field experience of thought, observations, data collection, and emotion in their field notebooks. Doing so can help students recognize that measurements made on a warm and sunny spring day can have a fundamentally different level of reproducibility than those taken in freezing, windblown sleet in early winter. Furthermore, thorough preparation and organization is required to conduct a successful field campaign. The field notebook is at the heart of this preparation, serving to coordinate electronic digital photography, data collection, and careful personal observation. Each page of the field notebook should be digitally photographed as it is completed, and then stored as backup copies each evening as the student summarizes and checks the notes. The field notebook further acts as a comprehensive diary, in which ideas, conversations, contacts, and memorable experiences are recorded. Interleaving words, phrases, and songs from foreign languages of the countries where they are studying with their scientific work is an essential means by which students reconstruct the details of their fieldwork when they are back in the university classroom and laboratory.

These approaches demonstrate, in the context of the field, that a dynamic synergy exists between geoscience education and systems geobiology research. This serves to illustrate at the onset that teaching and research are synchronized and inextricably linked efforts. Further, the field is an extremely well-suited venue to show that both teaching and research are required to enhance society through a better understanding of complex global feedback interactions between the geosphere and biosphere. In addition, the entire life-Earth system evolved prior to and independent of the establishment of political borders, making earth science a fundamentally international activity. The international global stage plays out through integrated learning experiences in classrooms, laboratories, and field sites around the world, where ongoing experimentation in nature demands that students use cross-disciplinary and cross-cultural scientific approaches. This in turn places students in fascinating yet totally unfamiliar natural environments. This holistically encourages the evaluation and application of "analogy identifies anomaly," in which students are required to regard the natural world through the objective lens of international perspectives. The field-based viewpoint thus creates cross-disciplinary learning environments that reflect scientific and cultural diversity, all within the framework of global earth science education.

I first began teaching classes in the field when I was in graduate school, where I led departmental courses to sites in the Caribbean in which I was conducting my dissertation research. This continued during my postdoctoral years, where the opportunities for integrated field instruction expanded to sites across North and South America, Europe, North Africa, Russia, and Ukraine. The central importance of extensive planning for the field, coupled with the need for constant strategic flexibility, proved especially vital on many occasions when bringing Dutch, Russian, and U.S. students on trips to the Crimean peninsula and the Austrian, French, and Italian Alps. Since I became a faculty member at the University of Illinois, the opportunity to offer field courses in these locations has continued and further expanded to include the Arctic. Throughout, I have observed how geology and the natural environment play central roles in all cultures, ethnic backgrounds, and nationalities. Thus, these experiences have been critical in the ongoing evolution of my own teaching approaches and made me acutely aware of the sensitive cultural and philosophical issues confronting the natural sciences and our global civilization as a whole.

I annually take students to Curaçao coral reefs (fig. 2) and Yellowstone hot springs. Students initially develop a detailed working knowledge about these sites during a semester of classroom lectures and laboratory experiments, which culminates with a capstone field experience. In the Curaçao course

FIGURE 2. Bruce Fouke teaching coral reef geobiology to University of Illinois students on the southern Caribbean island of Curaçao. Field photograph by Colleen Cook.

we stay at and work out of the Caribbean Research and Management of Biodiversity Institute (Carmabi). Here students utilize SCUBA and snorkel techniques to examine the modern coral reef tract underwater, comparing its ecosystem diversity, sedimentology, and chemistry with 16 million-year-old Miocene reef counterparts fossilized in the mountains along the leeward coast of the island. In Yellowstone, students learn winter mountaineering skills to conduct hands-on experiments in the field to test hypotheses they have formulated during the semester regarding the influence of heat-loving microbes on mineral precipitation.

The following quotation is from the field notebook of a student on one of the Curaçao coral reef trips. The notebook entry dramatically illustrates how students gain in-depth scientific knowledge while fully experiencing and connecting with the sublime natural environment in which they are working. These students have learned not only how to make and record scientific observations, but also how to integrate this knowledge with their own human experience and then transform that vision into words.

> The crystal clear jet black night sky had unveiled itself to us as a galactic roadmap of infinite proportions. We were now humbled before the magnitude of the celestial unknown, somewhat safe on a limestone precipice that is periodically shuddered by the impact of rolling surf. As if collectively enthralled by an ancient shared dream, we came to understand this place as the helm of a great ship called Earth, hurdling us forward on a journey that was billions of years in the making. The rocks comprising our current vantage point had come into existence many tens of millions of years ago as deep-water spreading center seafloor basalts in the southern Pacific Ocean. Tectonic forces then wrenched these deposits thousands of kilometers to the east, dragging them along the jagged northern margin of the South American plate. In the process, the rocks beneath our feet were uplifted more than half a kilometer, raising them from the permanent darkness of the deep oceanic abyss to the shallow seawater zone of sunlight penetration. Here, coral reefs would thrive for tens of millions of years and the present island of Curaçao would come into existence as part of the Lesser Antilles. As tectonic forces continued to uplift the island, sea level was independently driven up and down hundreds of meters as ice age glaciers on far away high-latitude continents waxed and waned. The combination of these multiple geological and biological processes created the coral reef limestone cliffs from which our view of the Caribbean sky show was now being witnessed. We now also see the same coastal marine environments in which we have been SCUBA diving earlier today, which allowed us to study the living reefs of this island.

The future of cross-disciplinary science demands that we train students to address the complex global environmental issues facing our society. An essential means to attain this goal is to ensure that at least some portion of their scientific education takes place in natural environmental settings. Field-based education gives students the experience of observing, documenting, and tracking natural processes, which develops their capacity for scientific inquiry while simultaneously fully engaging their senses and emotional intellect to develop a deeply personal sense of the Earth. Provided with these perspectives, future natural scientists will be delighted, surprised, informed, and ultimately educated by the environment itself each and every time that they step into a new natural surrounding.

COLLABORATIVE ARTISTS
How to Speak and Listen at the Same Time

Julie Jordan Gunn
School of Music

I am a musician, a collaborative pianist, someone who most enjoys the creative process of working and performing with others—singers, instrumentalists, composers, poets, dancers, and actors. For me, the challenge of being creative is best met as a team. I don't believe in the myth of the lone artist. Most of my growth, and most of my students' growth, has been through collaboration.

To understand my own artistic development, I think of the performing that meant the most to me. My main professional partner is also my husband, Nathan Gunn; while we have both collaborated with others in recital, our principal work is as a pair.

Our New York recital debut was at Weill Hall, with Schubert's *Die Schöne Müllerin*. This traditional recital offered a series of songs by the acknowledged father of German lieder. This recital demonstrated that we had become quite competent, but we weren't yet creative. We weren't yet able to perform from our unique points of view.

Having made the big debut, we made progress quickly, in the form of a recital of American songs ranging from folk songs to high art, arranged to tell the story of a man's life. American singers and pianists have been presenting American songs at the end of recitals for generations, but for this particular recital we introduced a slight innovation by disregarding the boundaries of genre, for example, by treating a pop song as if it had the same potential as an art song to convey a man's experience.

In our next venture, we combined Olivier Messiaen's twentieth-century avant-garde meditations on the Infant Jesus with the songs of fifth-century Irish monks, video, and modern dance, on the premises that dance could yield insights into the silent world of the monastery and that video images could take the place of the traditional program. After that we did a residency at New York's legendary Café Carlyle, combining jazz standards, cowboy songs, and lots of personal stories. Recently, the stage combination of Mandy Patinkin's "Singin' in the Bathtub" and Nathan's Barber of Seville, kicking off a high-energy romp through pop tunes, art songs, somber reflections on the Gettysburg address, and hit Broadway duets, has taken the juxtaposition of worlds and personalities to a new height.

As I've gained in confidence, the combinations in my performances have become more varied. As I've gained courage to explore new worlds, I've learned more about my own artistry and been able to define more sharply my own artistry. I believe that this process of exploration works for my students, as well.

Although creativity is very important to me, I can't imagine creating something out of nothing—there are too many possibilities to ever narrow anything down—so for me, intersections are a way to begin. I find that my best work comes from combining things—different instruments, styles, genres, and people. This isn't important to me just artistically, but also as part of life generally. Collaboration in small groups is how we learn to speak for ourselves, and listen to others (at the same time!) and to find common ground. And that sort of collaboration is a microcosm of a larger kind: the collaboration between the creators of art, the performers, and the audience. Specializing in small-group collaboration has made me a better artist, in that I have been encouraged by my collaborators to more fully articulate my own artistic ideas, and to more fully understand theirs. It has made me a better person, too, for the same reasons: I can speak and listen better in all contexts, not just artistic ones.

One way of understanding the creative process in the performance of music is to look at the way musicians organize themselves. In the classical music world, we organize ourselves in three ways. The first way is in the large ensemble: orchestras, operas, choruses. These groups are so large that they must have a leader speak for them. They are also so hierarchical that the leader is often called Maestro, Italian for "teacher," instead of by his or her name. Often the group stands when the leader enters the room. Orchestras have a level of formality almost unrecognizable in modern life. The players are ranked by ability and sit accordingly, with the principal player in each section sitting in the front and outside. This structure makes for highly efficient and well-coordinated playing because the performers can be responsive to the Maestro's wishes as expressed by his or her baton. They follow the "authoritative" model.

At the other extreme is the lone artist: the solo pianist or cellist who practices alone for six or seven hours daily, a solitary figure whose artistic ideas are so specific that they know no compromise. These players start from an early age to hold themselves to the most exacting standards. Their performances, both live and recorded, are compared to others, modern and historical—reviewers and fans notice differences in sound quality, articulation, tempo, pitch and rhythmic accuracy, and overall interpretation, all in excruciating detail.

In the middle, which is where I usually find myself, is the small group, anywhere from a duo to a quintet. With groups of this size, ranging from the art song recital for piano and voice to a piano quintet, a leader isn't essential. Each artist comes prepared to communicate his or her thoughts, and the rehearsal unfolds in a process of finding consensus. Leadership is handed off seamlessly and often without thought or a word uttered. In the ultimate collaborative group, the string quartet, the members play almost as one instrument. Some members may be outgoing, others more introverted. And an extroverted personality doesn't necessary imply extroverted music making. The social personality and the artistic personality can be totally different. But the total artistic product is more than the sum of the parts. Four people speak with one voice.

This should not be confused with democracy. A piano trio can't vote on the tempo in order to choose the one that two members like. The third member must be considered . . . he or she must come to feel that the choices make sense to him artistically. There is no compromise, only persuasion and consensus. If, over time, consensus becomes harder and harder to reach, it's more likely the trio will dissolve rather than ask a member to play in a manner that doesn't reflect his or her genuine artistic choices.

These levels of organization describe one system of collaboration: the collaboration between performers. A second system of collaboration is inherent in all the performing arts: the three-way collaboration between the creative team, the performers, and the audience. This three-legged structure is inherent to all performing arts. Demographics don't matter: A man from eighteenth-century Vienna writes a song based on a poem by a seventeenth-century Italian man. It is performed by a young woman from inner-city Chicago in the twenty-first century at a party attended by Asian immigrants, and somehow everyone understands. This is a miracle.

Both systems of music collaboration—the one between colleagues, and the second between performers, creators, and the audience—that exist in the artistic field can be easily adapted to the educational field. It is my privilege to teach our advanced students, who don't need as much physical or technical advice as their classmates and who already speak the musical language—its grammar, so to speak—and who instead need help defining their musical thoughts.

Each of us has a point of view, and that point of view is highly developed in artists. We continue to develop it throughout our lives, but students aren't yet independent. They must spend much more time and energy developing their own point of view, and need help to do it. This complicates the "musical negotiating" inherent to all artistic collaborations. How can you understand your colleague's point of view when he or she doesn't even understand it, or doesn't have one at all?

I address this developmental issue with three successive teaching approaches, each tailored for a particular stage of artistic understanding. The first is authoritative. Two students, a pianist and a soprano, come into a lesson with an aria from Mozart's *The Marriage of Figaro*, an opera with a story Lorenzo DaPonte adapted from Beaumarchais's trilogy about the social changes of the Enlightenment. They have dutifully learned the notes and rhythms, and the singer pronounces the Italian correctly. I review the language word for word—what's happening here? Susanna is dressing her friend Cherubino as a girl, but he won't keep still. I show them how Mozart's music is gentle and lyrical at first—Susanna is patient with the wiggly boy—although the trills in the left hand describe his fidgeting. Why does the music become more insistent? Is Susanna losing patience with the boy? Are the piano and vocal line always indicative of the same mood, or could they be expressing two (or three?) different characters? Other questions—is Cherubino an innocent child? Are they aware that in Beaumarchais's third play the Countess Almaviva has a child out of wedlock by this young man?

The teacher takes the creative team's role and shares what he or she imagines Mozart, DaPonte, or Beaumarchais would say were they present. I have developed a relationship with these long-dead composers that over the years, through many different works and collaborators. I can share that relationship with our students—"When Shostakovich writes an accent, it sounds like this" or "In Schubert's writing, appoggiaturas often make more sense if they sound longer." But yet—a good teacher encourages an individual interpretation. It is our job to find consensus between the student (and we want them to have strong views!), the creative team (who usually are not there to defend themselves), and the audience (experienced or inexperienced) who must be engaged in the work.

Having developed specific opinions, we can introduce a second teaching approach: role-playing. My colleague Stephen Taylor and I co-teach our most collaborative class, Songwriting. We start with existing American songs from Stephen Foster to Samuel Barber. The students take turns playing the piano, singing, and listening. But what makes this class special is that, every three weeks, students present their own work: their poetry, their composition, and their own performances. It is our belief that playing different roles makes students experience songs differently: the performers develop empathy for the composers, the composers for the poets, and the creative team for the performers.

A Korean American student shares a poem about her experience as two different people—as a "normal" American kid who wants to run around playing with her friends outside—and as the privileged daughter of an influential man, obliged to sit quietly in formal clothing at meetings while the other children play. Her classmate has set this poem as a duet between the two selves, with a more raucous style for the "normal" kid and a more restrained style for the "formal kid." A pianist and two singers perform for their classmates, who have questions—is the language too symbolic for non-Koreans to understand? Do the vocal differences between the two singers make it difficult for listeners to see them as two sides of the same person? Can we introduce a refrain to repeat the message for emphasis and clarity? The audience is the test: are we communicating? In our class, the audience will tell you right away.

The third approach I use, with the most advanced students, is teaching them how to teach, for many students aspire to be teachers or coaches. The act of teaching someone else can be powerfully instructive to the teacher. In order to convince someone else to adopt another point of view, our ideas must be clear and strong. It is extraordinarily challenging for students to learn how to sharpen and strengthen their own ideas, and it demands that they prepare more thoroughly than they ever have before.

If my coaching student wants to learn to teach a Debussy song on a Verlaine poem, he has a lot of work to do! First he must understand the French text and learn how to pronounce it correctly. He must then play Debussy's score, understanding Debussy's relationship with Verlaine's poetry. I will sing with him, so he can practice responding to me. Next, we switch: I play the piano while he sings the vocal part. This opens up all sorts of understanding for him. He literally understands the singer's point of view. He runs out of breath when it's too slow. He can't get all the words out if it's too fast. The result is that he'll be more sensitive in the future.

Now, armed with this knowledge and experience, he invites a classmate, a singer, into the studio. She's nervous about singing for us. This is an unfamiliar song, and although she knows she needs advice, she worries that she won't be able to please us. He listens for a while as she sings, and offers his first piece of advice. He corrects her French diction—she sometimes mispronounces the vowels. She nods and tries again, but it sounds the same to him. He starts to wonder, "Am I repeating myself?" He asks himself if he's not clear, or if he's maybe wrong about the vowels, and she's just being polite. He wonders if he'll discourage her by insisting. I speak to him later, encouraging him to stick to his guns about the vowels not being right. I encourage him to try rephrasing his suggestion until his language triggers an understanding in her.

He won't work this out in just one coaching. But he has begun to consider musical detail and communication more seriously. He's scratched the surface of the complex relationships that are informed by experience levels, talents, and personality. It will be a long journey.

Like that student, I learn from teaching. I am constantly challenged by putting myself in someone else's shoes. Each student gives me a new opportunity to practice seeing a score from another person's point of view, which then sheds new light on the score. I continue to refine my ideas about different works of art. In playing the role of the audience, I grow closer to the composers.

Some of the students are on the cusp of a musical career. Often they need confirmation that I also hear what they think is special about their work. With more unformed students, I am challenged to discern what is special about them artistically, often before they have done so themselves. When that happens, the understanding of others that I gain is its own reward.

The musical scores only live through the performers, each of which is different. Viewing the music through the lenses that my students provide makes me a better performer and strengthens my relationship with the composers and poets who gave me these miraculous scores. I hope to set my students on paths that allow them to bring their own special understanding to these scores, keeping them alive for generations to come.

THE INTIMATE UNIVERSITY
"We Are All in This Together"

Nancy Abelmann
Departments of Anthropology, Asian American Studies,
and East Asian Languages and Cultures

I am putting the finishing touches on this chapter after wrapping up my fall 2012 course, the Ethnography of Contemporary East Asia. I couldn't be happier with the six podcasts that my twenty-three students produced. As I guided the student teams in the making of these ten-minute, interview-based portraits of Chinese or South Korean international undergraduates, I was able to convey to them why anthropology is so exciting to me and what I find so intellectually compelling about studying "Korea" on my own campus. I designed the podcast assignment in relation to the course's focus on globalization, youth, migration, and social transformation in East Asia. I envisioned that through interviews with University of Illinois international undergraduates, students in the class could both experience these trends first-hand, and practice the methods of anthropology by constructing portraits and making arguments on the basis of interviews. The podcast assignment made particular sense at the University of Illinois because we have the largest number of international undergraduates among all U.S. public universities (over four thousand in 2012–13, with the vast majority coming from China and South Korea). The assignment also allowed me to introduce students to some of my own research, as I am engaged in a collaborative project on the University of Illinois as a contact zone in relation to this changing undergraduate student demography (the American University Meets the Pacific Century, AUPC).

One of the podcasts focused on a South Korean international student who was struggling with her inability to master English to a level where she could confidently imagine a future for herself in the United States. In the students' one-page essay introducing the podcast, which they titled "Crossing the Invisible Line," they reflected on the student this way: "Unable to overcome these [cultural] barriers, she is unable to 'get' jokes, and thus not sure about crossing that cultural bridge between American and Korean culture. . . . [She] seemed to have nearly given up because of segregation and tensions between American and international students." I asked each team to select an image to accompany the essay and the podcast; this team chose a photo of the gorgeous atrium in the new, state-of-the-art Business Instructional Facility. They wrote that they chose the image because "It could be one of the places where she both gains from participating in an American college experience as well as a place where she might experience segregation between groups of people. We wanted to express the tension she might feel between learning a lot at the U of I and still feeling like she was missing out on something."

The work of making a podcast, in this case one built on oral-history interviews, offers a wonderful model for the ethnographic method at the heart of sociocultural anthropology. Ethnography—namely qualitative research in which anthropologists conduct interviews, make observations, and often spend extended periods of time in the "field"—yields huge amounts of data, with its field notes, interview transcriptions, and reflections. Anthropologists make claims about our world on the basis of this ethnographic evidence, choosing from that extensive data evocative moments that best capture social reality—be they glimpses from a day, tidbits of conversation, or revealing stories. To cull ten minutes from two to three hours of audiotape required the students to think hard about what their podcast would "argue" and about how to achieve that argument most elegantly. One student from the "Crossing the Invisible Line" team reflected on the process eloquently: "Even after the interview, I wondered how much of a coherent story we could draw from the long and somewhat scattered interview. . . . But it was during the process of editing down the podcast when I learned the most from this exercise . . . the assignment forced us to find the heart of the tension and progression in our interviewee's story. We found that she struggled a lot with self-expression in the U.S. . . . When we isolated the main tension in her interview, it was easy and fun to edit down the recording to a ten-minute podcast that brought this tension to light."[1]

This sort of editing, arguing, and evoking teaches students how to read ethnography inside out, which is always my teaching goal, namely, to encourage students to actively think about how ethnographic arguments are composed through interpretation of the evidence, and to consider whether the same findings could support different arguments.

This course, like many I teach, is intimately tied to my own research as an anthropologist of transnational Korea. Indeed, for over twenty years I have focused both on South Korea and on diasporic Koreans in the United States.

Nearly uncannily, my own research career has been profoundly affected by the ways in which South Korea has come to life locally, at the University of Illinois and in the towns of Urbana and Champaign. Although I travel yearly to South Korea and have spent many extended periods there, it is not an exaggeration to say that I can feel the pulse of South Korean society right here at home because of the large numbers of South Koreans who find their way to our university. These days, scholars across the humanities and social sciences refer to the "global-local" to describe the ways in which it is nearly impossible to think about either the "local" or the "global" as distinct from one another. This is certainly the case for South Korea and Korean America.

A confession is in order: in my case it is not only that the classroom is a place that can productively enliven my areas of research interest, but that *many of my research interests have in fact emerged from the classroom.* I arrived at the University of Illinois in 1990 as an ethnographer of South Korea with a newly minted dissertation on South Korean social movements. Typical of area studies scholars at that time, I had by then taken pains to learn the Korean language and I was content to think about East Asia "over there." But little did I know that I had made my way to what was already the Unites States's top study-abroad destination for South Korean graduate students—East Asia was here! And by the mid-2000s, South Koreans began coming to the University of Illinois for their undergraduate degrees; these undergraduates are the students who were interviewed for the podcasts. These international Korean students joined the sizable number of Korean Americans (largely the second-generation children of immigrants) who have, for over two decades, been a presence at the university. My research interests in "Korea" at the University of Illinois began with these Korean Americans.

I learned quickly that although the Chicago-area Korean Americans in my classes were (somewhat) interested in the goings-on in the Koreas, they particularly wanted to make sense of their parents' emigration. So, in 1992 I taught a course that took up the Koreas and their diaspora—in the United States, China, Japan, Russia and the former Soviet republics, and Latin America. What I could have never predicted was what would happen late that spring semester: the Los Angeles riots on April 29. Korean Americans figured prominently in those riots as shopkeepers whose small businesses were looted or destroyed in the aftermath of the acquittal of four white Los Angeles Police Department officers accused of beating Rodney King, a black motorist whose beating had been videotaped and subsequently circulated widely.

With hindsight, we would learn that there were many other racial and ethnic groups of shopkeepers in Los Angeles, but at the time the most prominent images were of Korean émigré shopkeepers, some of whom were pictured guarding their shops in near-vigilante fashion. As it turned out, I was unprepared to help my students understand these events—events that really mattered to them as many were the children of Chicago shopkeepers who in every way resembled the Korean small-business owners in Los Angeles. That course became the seed of a book that I coauthored with John Lie, *Blue Dreams: Korean Americans and the Los Angeles Riots* (1995). Conducting the research for that book, I learned about the considerable class divides within the Korean American community between, for example, middle-class immigrants who had settled decades earlier, and recent working-class immigrants. I saw that how a Los Angeles Korean immigrant thought about the Rodney King decision and the subsequent riots was shaped in large part by his or her own history of immigration.

Through the research for *Blue Dreams*, I began to appreciate the diversity of the Korean American students in my classes. I remember one set of cousins in the same class: the daughter of a middle-class, educated father who emigrated in the 1970s; and the son of his much younger and uneducated brother who had remained in the South Korean countryside and emigrated in the 1990s. Interested in just this sort of diversity, in 1997 I began an ethnographic project on Korean Americans at the University of Illinois, with a focus on their lives and educational trajectories in relation to their parents' educational and immigration histories. That was also the same year in which I gave birth to twins, so it made sense to bring my research home. Conducting the research for the book that emerged, *The Intimate University: Korean American Students and the Problems of Segregation* (2009), transformed my writing and teaching. Determined to write a short and accessible book that could speak to undergraduates, I became increasingly committed to welcoming undergraduates to the table as researchers in their own right.[2] This project got me thinking about how many of my colleagues and I had been teaching ethnographic methods, namely by simply using the university as a "laboratory" in which students can try their hand at fieldwork. In 2002, this insight, with the invaluable help of an enthusiastic colleague, William Kelleher, led to the cofounding of the Ethnography of the University Initiative (EUI, www.eui.uiuc.edu), a pedagogical project through which students conduct and archive independent research on the university. The course I describe in this essay is affiliated with EUI, and my students presented their podcasts at the fall 2012 EUI conference.

However, in the years immediately following the 2009 publication of *The Intimate University*, what it meant to be a Korean American at the University of Illinois was transforming before my eyes. This transformation inspired me to begin the aforementioned new collaborative project, the American University Meets the Pacific Century, together with colleagues Soo Ah Kwon, Tim Liao, and Adrienne Lo. We run the project as a social science research laboratory. As I write this essay, AUPC is about to begin its fifth semester, with some twenty undergraduate and graduate students. Students in the AUPC lab each choose a project, and we train them in the methods of the social sciences: they conduct original research, archive their field notes, and transcripts, and make presentations based on their work. Some students have used this research for senior honors theses, and some have plans to publish. The book that will someday emerge from this project will feature the findings of many undergraduate researchers.

At the beginning of my fall 2012 course, the Ethnography of Contemporary East Asia, students read interview transcripts from AUPC as well as read a recently published article of mine that examines the often-tense relationship between South Korean international undergraduates and second-generation Korean Americans (2012). In that article, I examine the tensions between Korean Americans who sometimes think of South Korean international students as "rich and spoiled" kids who are able to cash in on a U.S. college degree without any of the sacrifices that come with growing up in immigrant families; and South Korean students who sometimes think of Korean Americans as having forsaken their language and culture, but who also wonder why they are not fully integrated in U.S. society. I could tell that it was illuminating for the students who interviewed South Korean international students for their podcast to witness firsthand the conflicts that I described in my article.

The podcast project managed to bring scholarship to life. One student's reflections speak to this: "It provided us a unique opportunity to actually collect firsthand data to reflect on and 'test' the class readings. I imagine that authors we have read would be kind of 'anxious' if they knew what we do in this class. As I was doing the annotated version of the transcript, it came to me that, 'OMG [Oh my God], I can almost link all readings we have read in this course to this transcript in some way.'" For this student, contemporary East Asia had come to life through the interview, as had the scholarly process. This is a professor's dream: to have students come to appreciate scholars' attempts to understand the human experience.

I close this chapter with a description of a podcast that prominently featured an interviewee's revelation, one that fascinated the team members. The interviewee said this during her interview: "At first, I thought that there are more freedoms here in America, everything looks so different, and everyone looks like they know they can do whatever they wanna do, but now I'm thinking it's about same here and Korea. Now I figured out that some people actually have to follow their parents' rule, go through the school's rule . . . I guess that's same all over the world." The student interviewer followed up: "So, are you disappointed about that?" And the interviewee replied, "No, actually I'm happy to find out that, because first I felt like I am the only one who can't enjoy the freedom. But now I know that everyone has to follow the same thing. So I feel a lot better." The team decided to name their podcast, "It Doesn't Matter Where I Live: Everyone Has to Follow the Same Thing." For their accompanying image they searched Google Images for "citizen of the world," and in their essay introducing the podcast they describe their reasons for the image they chose:

> We ended up choosing an image of a group of people of various nationalities holding up a huge globe; it appears to be a photo taken of a statue. We felt that this was appropriate because Grace sees the world as a place with a vast number of interesting and unique cultures, but she also sees it as a place where no one is perfectly "free." Thus the burden of supporting the globe in the statue reflects the universal burden that everyone must carry. Yet the image does not seem oppressive; there is nothing to indicate that the people holding up the globe are about to fail or are about to be crushed. It is important to note this, since Grace's message was not one of despair. She no longer feels that there is some panacea of freedom that a lucky few have access to while she is denied it. She can stop seeing the grass as always greener in America and fully enjoy the less-than-perfect greenness that exists everywhere in the world.

They concluded their essay with these words: "For Grace there is a way in which 'we are all in this together.'"

That the students in my class could both learn about the specificity of young East Asians' educational sojourns abroad and contemplate the perhaps shared predicament of all youth today is more than I could have ever dreamed of as a teacher. The teaching and research feedback loop has been a great ride for me; happily, I am still on board.

ACKNOWLEDGMENTS

In preparing this essay, I am grateful for conversations with Dana Rabin, and for the editorial wisdom and generosity of Kathy Brenner, Nicole Constable, Maria Gillombardo, Nicole Newendorp, Sumie Okazaki, Dana Rabin, Eun Hee Emily Ryo (who was an undergraduate in my classes in the early

1990s), and Erica Vogel. I would also like to thank the fabulous steward-ship of Antoinette and Mary-Ann: I have benefited from both their clear vision for this book and their editorial generosity. Finally, I am grateful to Carol Spindel, my *Sampler* discussant, for her wise and beautifully penned response to the first version of this essay.

NOTES

1. Students archived their podcasts together with both documentation on and reflections about the process of making the podcast.

2. To date, over 1,700 undergraduates have engaged in this research in over a hundred EUI classes across dozens of departments, building archives of over 1,200 student research projects in IDEALS (Illinois Digital Environment for Access to Learning and Scholarship), the University of Illinois's digital repository (https://www.ideals.illinois.edu/handle/2142/755, accessed November 9, 2013).

WORKS CITED

Abelmann, Nancy. 2009. *The Intimate University: Korean American Students and the Problems of Segregation*. Durham, N.C.: Duke University Press.

Abelmann, Nancy. 2012. "Undergraduate Korean Americans and 'Korean Koreans' in the Millennial American University." In *Koreans in America: History, Culture and Identity*, edited by Grace J. Yoo, 109–17. San Diego: Cognella Academic Publishing.

Abelmann, Nancy, and John Lie. 1995. *Blue Dreams: Korean Americans and the Los Angeles Riots*. Cambridge, Mass.: Harvard University Press.

Painting with Numbers (and Shapes, and Symmetry)

Jayadev Athreya
Department of Mathematics

> A mathematician, like a painter or a poet, is a maker of patterns.
> If his patterns are more permanent than theirs, it is because they
> are made with ideas.
> —G. H. Hardy

What do you think mathematics is? A body of facts: static, majestic, imposing, and intimidating? Is it to be learned in a series of increasingly difficult stages, from the base camp of arithmetic to the intermediate peaks and traverses of high school algebra and geometry, to the mountaintops of calculus, analysis, abstract algebra, and topology in college? Do we abandon those who stumble along the way, shaking our heads sadly at those who stumble? "If you struggled this much with trigonometry, how will you handle calculus?"

What do you think mathematical research is? A stately march up these mountains, exploring ever more complicated phenomena? Adding larger and larger numbers, as it were? And while the prose may be overwrought, this is how many within even our academic culture perceive the discipline of mathematics—the hardest of hard sciences, a diamond edge.

This, as any practicing research mathematician can tell you, is utterly insane. In his Swiftian essay "The Mathematician's Lament," the research-mathematician-turned-high-school-teacher Paul Lockhart compared this model of mathematics and its teaching in our schools and universities to a society that *seems* to value proficiency in art (requiring good art grades, for example, to get into college) but that in practice teaches art by rote.[1] Art class involves first learning the *theory* of art, so when students finally do paint, they tend to paint by numbers, so to speak. The focus of the curriculum is not on applying paint to canvas but rather on applying the theory to the real world—more like painting your house than creating a work of art.

Circulated in the mathematics community, Lockhart's essay resonated because what we do is *creative art*, and that this is not at all reflected in the way our society perceives it, or, in fact, the way we as a profession teach it. We don't encourage children to explore and discover, and make mistakes, and play with mathematics, which denies them knowledge of what actual mathematics is. By focusing only on the most utilitarian aspects of arithmetic, we deny people the opportunity to access and discover vast swathes of creative beauty.

Mathematics is an art like music, or painting, or sculpture, where practitioners create, for beauty's sake (and often no other reason). Just as music is the art of patterns of sound, *mathematics is the art of creation and study of abstract patterns*. Mathematicians practice their art by playing and exploring with abstract, but natural, objects.

For example, my research is in geometry. This doesn't mean I spend my time doing the dreaded column-based T-proofs of high school. What I do is in many ways much less arcane—I think about how to fold and glue various shapes into interesting surfaces, and how to measure distances on the result. For example, if you take a rectangle and glue the top and the bottom, you get what looks like a poster tube. If you then glue the ends of the tube, you get what's called a torus, or more prosaically, a tire. You can think of the classic computer game Pac-Man as being played on such a surface, for every time he disappears off the top, he reemerges from the bottom (gluing the top to the bottom), and every time he goes off the side, he reemerges from the other side (gluing the left to the right).

I study (among other things) what happens if you play a similar gluing game on an octagon, or other kinds of shapes, and what happens if we speed up our Pac-Man figure in certain directions and slow him down in others.

What I'm doing here is *playing*. I'm not doing this for any deeper reason than to try to find common (and often beautiful) patterns. For instance, it turns out, roughly speaking, if Pac-Man on the square starts along a straight-line path (assuming that our Pac-Man can also travel along any line he wants) that never returns him to where he started, then, eventually, the amount of time he spends in any particular region during his travels depends only on the total area of the region. In a joint paper, my coauthor and I show that this happens quickly, for many kinds of polygonal boards folded into surfaces.[2]

So, if mathematicians are (at least in part) creative artists and humanists, why don't we all teach like creative artists? Why would any of us teach by rote, painting-by-numbers? Why instead don't we teach painting *with* numbers (and shapes, and symmetry); why don't we teach by doing?

Before arriving at the University of Illinois, I had rarely taught the *doing* of mathematics. Even for my most advanced mathematics students, I stuck to fixed subjects, developed a fixed syllabus, and was always concerned about certain benchmarks. Mostly, I taught calculus and linear algebra, faithfully trying to make sure my students could do the problems, despairing when they couldn't.

In my first semester in Urbana in the fall of 2010, I had the opportunity to teach an advanced non-Euclidian geometry course for mathematics education majors. I worried they might only be taking my course to satisfy the State of Illinois advanced geometry requirement for high-school mathematics teachers. I feared they wouldn't care about the beauty of the subject. As it turned out, I couldn't have been more wrong. They were some of the best students I ever had.

In addition to building up their mathematical abilities, I tried to engage them in pedagogical questions, asking them to reflect on *how* they were learning the material as they progressed. The mechanism we used, suggested by colleagues, was journaling. Each student kept a journal, making weekly entries on topics and questions of my suggestion. Often, I would ask the students to describe in words the concepts we had been studying; sometimes I would ask how they would attempt to teach the material. Although my students may have encountered journaling in humanities classes, some were initially resistant to applying the practice in a mathematics course. The journaling assignment was basically an experiment in metacognition, that is, in thinking about thinking. The students warmed to the task quickly, and in course evaluations several students noted that they would have liked more journaling. While journaling was successful in getting the students to think about their way of learning, it was less effective in communicating why I fell in love with geometry, or that it was even possible to do so. I hadn't communicated to my students the sense of creative *play* that mathematics is for mathematicians. I had missed an opportunity.

That summer, I went to join my partner as she completed a year of anthropological fieldwork in northern India. In fact, as I write this chapter, I'm sitting on the balcony of the house where we stayed that summer, looking out in the distance at the Himalayan range. It was here that I learned to *really* teach. At the beginning of the summer, I volunteered to work with students and teachers at a kindergarten-through-fifth-grade school run by a local nongovernmental organization. Initially, I planned to just work with the teachers, mainly because I wasn't sure about my shaky skills in Hindi, the medium of instruction.

The teachers, however, pushed me straight into the classroom. Working closely with third-, fourth-, and fifth-graders, bumbling my genders and mixing my verbs, I realized that getting complicated words and concepts across just wasn't feasible. What I could do, however, was get the kids to play, to explore, and to come up with their own words, their own concepts. With the fifth-graders, for example, we started by looking at corners, by trying to fit various kinds of tiles (and even the tables they sat at) together, and looking around the room for different kinds of corners. This eventually led us to the concept of angle, and even of *measuring* angles, as a way to determine whether various kinds of corners could fit together. None of this exploration came down from above—rather, the concepts came from the children themselves, as and when they needed them. I would come home every day excited and fired up about mathematics.

My research program too was flourishing, with plenty of time to think and few distractions. I managed to understand *why* something I had earlier proved was true. I had been studying the shapes of *lattices*, or regular grids, on a flat plane, by trying to understand their behavior when they were sheared in a certain way. My coauthor and I had proved that under this shearing procedure, the lattices developed horizontal vectors at certain moments, and by studying carefully this sequence of moments, we could obtain a lot of information about the shapes of the lattices.[3] What I realized—in what seemed like a flash but what I knew was the culmination of hours of thinking and playing—was that what we were really looking at were the slopes of certain lines in the lattice, and crucially, that there was an underlying relationship that had nothing to do with the lattice structure, but rather had to do with slopes of lines. This insight allowed me to develop a new, more fully realized theory, because I was able to understand that the pattern we had perceived held in much greater generality than the lattice setting.[4] I don't believe the teaching and the research progress were unrelated. I had reminded myself, after quite a bit of time, to just let go and play, and to let the thoughts take me where they wanted to go.

After returning from the mountains to the prairie, as excited as I had ever been for an academic year, I was faced with a question: *Could an exploration-based strategy for teaching elementary school children, born out of a lack of language skill, apply to teaching advanced mathematics to college students?*

That fall, I taught two courses: an honors abstract algebra course, for some of the traditionally very best mathematics students at the University of Illinois; and my old standard, non-Euclidean geometry. Despite the very different student populations, I decided to teach the two classes in a similar fashion. I would stick to traditional (computer-based) lectures on Monday and Wednesday, but on Friday, I would "flip" the classroom—the students would work on a project in small groups, as I went from group to group to see how their brainstorming was going.

In retrospect, I almost wish I'd had the courage to do all the classes this way. Seeing the students innovate, teach each other, and rapidly eliminate errors via collaboration was a delight. The projects would often involve the students proving a highly nontrivial result, first by discovering what the result should be and then thinking about why it was true. Sometimes they didn't finish in the time allotted, but they pursued the loose ends with far greater passion than they would have an unfinished homework assignment.

This desire to see the students explore and collaborate is also the reason that I started the Illinois Geometry Lab, a facility that matches undergraduates with faculty having appropriate in-semester research projects. We helped assemble teams consisting of a faculty member, a graduate student, and a couple of undergraduates. The idea was to give undergraduates the opportunity to do the kind of open-ended exploration and play that make mathematics so attractive to us, by linking them with a vertically integrated team of mathematicians.

The lab, with its focus on mathematics with visual, computational, and physical components, has built on the traditional strengths of our department (our faculty have been at the forefront of connecting geometry and computation), and it has clearly tapped into something students want. In the 2013 spring semester, we had thirty-seven undergraduates participating in twelve projects, an extraordinary level of involvement in undergraduate research.

There are downsides to this exploration-based approach: in a course, you don't cover as much as the syllabus says you should. For an open-ended project, you may not get any results. College teachers are always asking each other "what did you cover this semester?," by which they usually mean "what information did you attempt to convey to the students from the front of the room?" That question is often the beginning of a lamentation about how little the students actually absorbed, and *it's altogether the wrong question.*

With the challenges we face from those who doubt the value of in-person instruction and interaction, we must move beyond the idea of education, in particular mathematical education, as the top-down dissemination of facts. We labor to race through a syllabus that every one of our pedagogical senses tell us is too long to acquire any mastery over, instead of giving our students opportunities to explore, discover, and push the boundaries of what they know.

We shouldn't be pointing out geographical features on a map, telling them "these are the mountains, this is the prairie." Instead, let's lead our students through the landscape, show them the cliffs and crags that make up the mountains, the passes and the valleys that lead us down, the tall grasses and wildflowers that make up the prairie.

NOTES

1. Paul Lockhart, *A Mathematician's Lament: How School Cheats Us Out of Our Most Fascinating and Imaginative Art Form* (New York: Bellevue Literary Press, 2009).

2. Jayadev Athreya and Giovanni Forni, "Deviation of Ergodic Averages for Rational Polygonal Billiards," *Duke Mathematical Journal* 144, no. 2 (August 2008): 285–319.

3. Jayadev Athreya and Yitwah Cheung, "A Poincaré Section for the Horocycle Flow on the Space of Lattices," *International Mathematics Research Notices* (2013).

4. The new theory is described in Jayadev Athreya, "Gap Distributions and Homogeneous Dynamics," *Proceedings of International Congress of Mathematicians Satellite Conference on Geometry, Topology, and Dynamics in Negative Curvature*, forthcoming.

From Desk to Bench
Linking Students' Interests to Science Curricula

Lauren A. Denofrio-Corrales
Honors Program in the College of Liberal Arts and Sciences

Yi Lu
Departments of Chemistry, Biochemistry, Bioengineering,
and Materials Science and Engineering

A first-year undergraduate student at the University of Illinois, majoring in chemistry, discovers through her new independence away from home that she loves cooking and baking. She begins to wonder about the changes she witnesses in food as she prepares it. For instance, when egg whites harden in the pan, why do they change from a transparent goop to a white solid? She hopes that her chemistry and biology teachers will cover some of her questions in class, considering how often she finds herself pondering about the science of food. But, by midsemester, her teachers haven't mentioned anything about food in either class. Unsure exactly how to proceed with her interests, she checks out a library book about the chemistry of cooking. It is dense and difficult to read, but she finds some of it interesting. She also attends a lecture about proteins (eggs have protein, she reasons), but given the introductory nature of her first-year classes in chemistry and biology, she is not yet equipped to understand much of the technical language used during the presentation. This student has everyday questions that require a technical, interdisciplinary scientific explanation. As she is beginning to understand, researchers at the frontiers of the scientific disciplines, indeed at the intersections of the scientific disciplines, are asking similar questions about her topic of interest: the chemistry and biology of food.

What this student needs in order to more deeply explore her interests is a bridge between her ordinary science classes (where she sits at the *desk*) and the world of scientific research (where she can explore her interests at the *bench*). As a researcher on the frontiers of chemistry and biology (Lu) and a chemistry teacher concerned with the attraction and retention of students to the science disciplines (Denofrio-Corrales), we sensed the disconnect between students' interdisciplinary interests and the content of the courses we co-taught. Co-teaching allowed us to form a partnership that has lasted over a decade and given us the opportunity to collaboratively work on this very issue. As scientist-teachers, we use our experiences from research practice to build a bridge for students, helping them go between the desk and the bench, and guiding them toward the best sources of information, academic courses, and research experiences to strengthen the link between individual interests and the traditional science curricula.

Learning Science at the Desk

Ten years ago, we asked roughly forty University of Illinois students majoring in physical or natural science fields a seemingly innocuous question—"What are your scientific research interests?" Most responses were cast in the hot areas of current scientific research—"cancer research" or "genetically modified foods" or "alternative energy sources." These undergraduates made up the first cohort of the Chemistry and Biology of Everyday Life (CBEL), a new chemistry course that links topics of everyday life like health, food, and energy to cutting-edge research studies in chemistry and biology. We hoped CBEL would create a bridge between desk and bench for a sliver of the students studying in the physical and natural sciences at our institution.

The first few semesters that CBEL was offered, we wanted to know what fascinated these undergraduates, vexed them, or got their curiosity thrumming away about topics that were rooted in their own experiences and in current scientific inquiry. We identified the curricula in introductory and intermediate major courses in chemistry and biology as centered on foundational concepts that were crucial to developing a solid understanding of the discipline but that gave students little insight into the research topics about which they were most passionate. We found a troubling gap between the content of sequential courses in a scientific major (such as Chem 101, 201, 301, and so on) and the students' actual scientific interests, most of which came from current, interdisciplinary research areas (Denofrio, Russell, Lopatto, and Lu, 2007).

How does this weak link manifest itself in the lives of undergraduates studying in physical and natural sciences? For instance, students who are interested in anticancer pharmaceuticals might never encounter the topic as a part of regular course content, or might have to take a host of courses before reaching a course that provides insight into cancer research or pharmaceutical drug design. Perhaps the wait for what is truly interesting is too difficult, or the content in the sequential courses too removed, for students to persist in their major. We do not mean to say that students will find the sequential courses in their majors unattractive, purposeless, or irrelevant. We believe, however, that their chronological structure (beginning with fundamental, historical scientific discoveries) and prescribed nature (often inflexible to consider the interdisciplinary nature of students' interests) can sometimes deter even the most tenacious undergraduates.

It remains extremely difficult to make a standard set of curricula in chemistry or biology that follow a prescribed pattern, build a foundation of concepts and skills, and also serve as a relevant and interesting primer to current research in the areas each individual student finds fascinating. Therefore, we tried to complement the existing curricula by introducing students early to the excitement of scientific discovery at the frontiers of science, and to build CBEL as a companion to a traditional major plan of study in biology or chemistry. We tried to create a course with a nonstandard curriculum that was defined and driven by the students' interests and that linked their everyday interests to current science research taking place at the University of Illinois and other institutions.

Learning to Be a Scientist at the Bench

Considering how to link students' interests and course curricula made us reflect on our own concepts of *teaching* and *research*, and indeed to rethink the notion of *learning* in science. Completing a science major in chemistry or biology with the goal of becoming a research scientist means traversing a sequential set of courses designed to provide a foundational body of knowledge and a relevant skill set for eventual work at the bench in a laboratory. This education model adopts a cognitive perspective of learning. This means that learning is framed (1) as absorbing knowledge provided by teachers and textbooks and (2) as constructing ideas about scientific phenomena by inquiry and discovery. Knowledge is assumed to exist as concepts that reside in the minds of the teacher and her or his students, and is transmitted to the student through a series of exercises in classrooms and teaching laboratories that constitute the overt curriculum.

Through reflection on our own practices as scientist and teacher, we recognized that becoming a research scientist involves much more. Learning *to be a scientist* involves more than learning *science*. Learning to be a scientist requires a kind of apprenticeship experience, where one assumes the skills, dispositions, beliefs, and values of other, more experienced scientists by participating in the practice of scientific research. Through such participation, undergraduates learn traditions of scientific discourse, the norms of the disciplinary community, and the unique culture of research scientists—a tacit collection of beliefs and practices in the research community. This kind of knowledge is situated, and is not discrete. One cannot learn it by reading a textbook or solving even the most difficult of classroom exercises. Instead, it is passed down from generation to generation as a kind of situated curriculum.

Therefore there exists a second troubling gap, this one between the overt curriculum of chemistry and biology courses and the situated curriculum of learning to be a scientist. That is to say, there is a gap between the two types of learning, one being cognitive, and located in sites of formal instruction, and the other being situated, and located in sites of informal instruction, where authentic research is practiced. Our experience of this gap, and our desire to close it, grew out of our work as mentors to graduate-student researchers and teachers. The graduate-school model is an apprenticeship model, where students learn by participating in the practices of research and teaching, in collaboration with master scientists, master teachers, and "journeymen"—other apprentices at various stages of development. Our own practices have shown us how important and effective an apprenticeship model can be in learning how to be a scientist.

We wanted to impart this type of learning in CBEL, and to facilitate access to undergraduate research opportunities of the highest quality for University of Illinois students in the physical and natural sciences. A major step in building a bridge between desk and bench is encouraging students to be deliberate about preparing for and finding a supportive research environment that matches their major interests. Therefore, we sought to scaffold students' efforts by providing a model of a scientific research group within the CBEL classroom. We structured the class into small, investigative teams, each consisting of an integrative group of students across all four years of study, with the junior/senior students serving as exemplary undergraduate researchers and peer mentors to first-year and sophomore, less experienced students.

Building a Bridge between Desk and Bench

With the support of Howard Hughes Medical Institute (HHMI), the Department of Chemistry at the University of Illinois offered the first Chemistry and Biology of Everyday Life (CBEL) as a pilot course for about forty students in 2002. CBEL was not envisioned as either an honors course or as a replacement for traditional courses; instead, it runs alongside the sequential curriculum of chemistry and biology. It is an information center, making other science courses more meaningful; a triage, where each student's background and interests are analyzed; a matchmaker, where students' interests are matched to instructional materials; and a forum, where students can interact with others who have common interests. Perhaps most importantly, our students describe it as a bridge between classroom and undergraduate research experiences in their majors.

Undergraduates at all levels enroll in CBEL, and they are encouraged to take it early in their college careers and then reenroll each spring term until they graduate. Junior/senior, more experienced students serve as peer mentors and facilitators for first-year/sophomore, less experienced students. Throughout the course, instructors and peer mentors help students to develop necessary skills to investigate their own interests through activities such as mini-literature reviews, special topics discussions, journal article assignments, visits to laboratories, and attendance at scientific meetings. All exercises and assignments provide scaffolding for building to the final assignment; all work is shared with and reviewed by peers and instructors along the way.

Our approach in CBEL is to script the curriculum around students' interests, providing the skills to connect their interests to cutting-edge research, and to model the situated curriculum of science research practice through peer mentoring and experiential learning. The course mirrors a research group: it is cut into specialized teams, multidisciplinary, interest-driven, and responsive to cutting-edge research. CBEL is an insider's look at how science research works and a training ground for framing, articulating, and executing high-level analysis in scientific research. CBEL strengthens both the apparent and the hidden weak link between students' interests and science curricula.

To strengthen the link between students' interests and the curricula of their traditional courses, CBEL uses students' interests to write the syllabus and drive the direction of the curriculum. Soon after their registration, students are asked to identify their research interests in science. Content lectures, tailored to students' self-identified interests, are scripted by instructors throughout the term and given once per week to provide the background and vocabulary necessary to understand and analyze current scientific literature related to their interests. Instructors also facilitate open sessions called skill lectures, where we introduce the tools and skills needed to be an effective research scientist.

To build a bridge between the classroom (learning at a desk) and the research laboratory (learning at the bench), CBEL models a scientific research group. Bringing together a diverse set of students of different ages, years-in-school, and overall college experiences, the class is cut into smaller teams by way of students' self-identified interests. The teams are called subgroups, much as they would be in a laboratory research environment. Each student is placed into a subgroup based on several criteria: his or her scientific interests, number of times in CBEL, and undergraduate research experience. The subgroup is specific to some subject or topic that encompasses the members' interests, such as forensics or pharmaceuticals or alternative energy. Less-experienced students use the subgroup as a site of informal learning. They ask questions about the situated curriculum of science: how to locate useful courses, how to enter a research laboratory, how to be successful as a researcher. Peer mentors transfer tacitly the values, assumptions, and beliefs that they have come to understand from their research experiences in a laboratory.

To *infuse excitement and interdisciplinary questions into science learning at the University of Illinois, CBEL hosts sessions with guest scientists, whole-class activities, and field trips.* Dialogue and discussion become commonplace in the CBEL classroom as students teach each other and welcome guest scientists who provide in-depth talks on current, cutting-edge research. A most exciting complement to traditional lecture, some scientists open their laboratory spaces for special CBEL tours. CBEL students have been fortunate to visit the Illinois Research Park, the Institute for Genomic Biology, the Beckman Institute, and many interdisciplinary research laboratories. We have also hosted field trips to industrial laboratories in Chicago, Indianapolis, and St. Louis and have accompanied our students to experience firsthand the excitement of scientific discovery at national professional conferences.

Strengthening the Bridge between Desk and Bench

In our ten years as scientist-teachers on this project, we have seen how CBEL complements, rather than competes with, existing sequential courses in science disciplines, such as chemistry or biology, by working tangentially with the traditional system. Dramatic, large-scale changes to traditional curriculum (even when they are informed by research) are often perceived as too costly and disruptive to implement. Therefore, we believe that CBEL is a possible interests-driven model for other research universities and in other disciplines. For example, why not create a Physics and Mathematics of Everyday Life course? The CBEL model is multidisciplinary. Such a course could also work to build the bridge and strengthen the links between classroom and research laboratory.

We also believe that there is a place for the CBEL philosophy within the traditional curriculum, and that even traditional curricula can take on an interests-driven perspective. In 2007, we moved successful CBEL modules into the mainstream chemistry curriculum with support from the University of Illinois Provost's Office. We called this module implementation the Chemistry Enrichment Project (CEP), and asked interested students to participate in extra mentoring and research-based activities. As in the standard version of CBEL, the CEP participants expressed enthusiasm for the activities and reported significant learning gains in research-related areas.

From our professional experiences, we have learned that to explore deeply individual interests, undergraduates need a bridge between ordinary science classes (the *desk*) and the scientific research laboratory (the *bench*). Rather than aiming to change the sequential model of science curricula, which remains an important foundation of undergraduate education, CBEL works in tandem with standard courses. We believe the future of undergraduate education lies in an interest-driven model that is widely portable across disciplines and can effectively and wholly integrate research and classroom experiences. As scientist-teacher partners, we seek to strengthen the link between individual interests and the traditional science curricula at the University of Illinois, by pointing the students toward the traditional courses that match their interests, making them more motivated to remain in science majors, and encouraging them to enter the research laboratory early in their undergraduate career.

REFERENCES

Denofrio, Lauren A., Brandy Russell, David Lopatto, and Yi Lu. 2007. "Linking Student Interests to Science Curricula." *Science* 318 (5858): 1872–73.
Lopatto, David. 2004. "Survey of Undergraduate Research Experiences (SURE): First Findings." *Cell Biology Education* 3 (4): 270–77.

Bringing Statistics to Life

Flavia C. D. Andrade
Department of Kinesiology and Community Health

It's a freezing Monday in January at 9 A.M. How to make a full class of students motivated to be here? The thermostat in the classroom, a large lecture hall, is set at 70°F, but many of my students are shivering, hesitant, and intimidated by the title of the class: Health Statistics. For many of them, statistics and mathematics are not their favorite subjects, but this is a required course for most of them. Some of them have had limited mathematics training in high school, which makes them apprehensive. Asking them on their first day of class how they feel about the course and about their expectations, I sense the anxiety in their responses:

> Numbers scare me.

> I am very nervous about this course because I am not good at math, at all.

As I stand in front of the students, I think about how much I love numbers—not numbers by themselves, but numbers that allow us to address some of the most compelling questions about health and well-being in global terms. In my research, I experience the capacity of numbers to transform our understanding of people's health in very concrete ways. I address the impact on Latinos' well-being in the United States and Latin America of changes in demographics (such as the increase in longevity), epidemiology (such as the shift in the leading cause of death from infectious and parasitic diseases to noncommunicable and degenerative ones), and nutrition (such as the increased intake of saturated fat and sugar, refined foods, and foods low in fiber). We know that we are living longer—between 1900 and 2009, life expectancy (the average number of years a person expects to live) in the United States increased from 47 to 78.5 years (National Center for Health Statistics, 2012). But how can we make these additional years *better* for people?

Without statistics, the answers to these questions are incomplete. It is true that the mathematical equations involved in statistics may be lifeless, but the numbers themselves carry meaning, and that is what I care about. In fact, since my undergraduate days I have been interested in how to compile massive amounts of data that would serve populations impacted by diabetes, obesity, and disability. This passion helped me as I studied economics, demography, sociology, and later public health. As a classroom teacher whose research illuminates how numbers can change policy, attitudes, and even lives, I try to convey to students that statistics are key to the public health field and that a strong grounding in numbers will equip them for both work and life in ways they can't anticipate. In this sense, my goal is to tap their initial curiosity and show them the kinds of rewards it can repay. When I hear them say things like "I think statistics will teach me how to tame [my fear for statistics], so I am kind of excited," I know they are on the road to seeing statistics not as an abstraction but as a part of a skill set they can draw on daily in various parts of their lives.

Living longer and better lives should be something everyone aspires to, and statistics can help us find identify ways to achieve this . . . but how can I transfer my enthusiasm for statistics to the new generation of college students and future scholars? I use four main strategies. First, I ask them to think about the number of times they come across numbers and statistics on a typical day. The results usually surprise them, as expressed by one student:

> I was skeptical at the idea of actually noting statistics throughout my day. I honestly was not convinced that I would encounter much evidence of this class in my daily life. It turns out that I was very wrong.

We come across statistics in websites, blogs, newspapers, magazines, scientific articles, social networking sites . . . and the list goes on. Statistics can be obtained through surveys, medical records, election polls, and website pop-up questions. I want to prepare students to be able to look critically at data and other types of statistical information to make informed assessments about the claims attached to them. I emphasize that while they have to know how to use equations, the task at hand is not memorization but critical interpretation of the data they are encountering.

Second, because I know that students feel more connected when focusing on issues that matter most to them, I encourage them to identify a topic related to their own interests that they would like to see addressed in class. This can be challenging because students come to my class from many disciplines: kinesiology, community health, speech and hearing, recreation, sport and tourism, political science, communication, and nutrition, among others. A kinesiology student may be interested in physical activity among peers—how many students are physically active and how many times they exercise vigorously during a week. Another student may be interested in dietary patterns—how many vegetables or portions of meat are consumed on a daily basis? Another student may raise a question on internet preferences—how many fellow students have a Facebook account, how many times they access it during a day. In assisting them with the development of their own question, I draw directly on my own interdisciplinary training, emphasizing that the common thread across all the areas of study on which public health touches is the use of statistics: mathematical models and computation techniques to analyze data in order to better understand the impact of, say, obesity on disability and public policy. In one of my studies, for example, I joined collaborators in examining the impact of obesity on disability and the impact of weight changes on health transitions related to disability in Brazil (Andrade et al., 2013). We found that individuals who were obese were more likely than those who were not obese to develop some severe forms of disability, such as the inability to eat or dress autonomously, and with lower recovery rates from mobility limitations. Brazil, like many other developing countries, has historically been mainly concerned with curbing malnutrition (Monteiro, Conde, & Popkin, 2007). Our findings have important implications for policy makers in Brazil with regard to curbing disability risk by promoting the use of effective preventive measures that target the marketing of unhealthy foods and sedentary behaviors.

Third, I engage students directly in my research process by using i>clickers. The i>clicker is one type of the many small, automatic response devices that allow for instant data collection from students, analysis, and sharing during class (Bruff, 2009). This is particularly important for giving a voice to students in a large class setting—between 70 and 140 students every semester in my course. We routinely collect data about class members and use it during class to model how to calculate different statistics depending on the topic of the class: mean, medians, standard deviations, confidence intervals among others. This direct involvement in the research process is an indispensable way to help students feel connected not only to the statistical topic, but also to the group to which they belong.

Fourth, because students come from many disciplines, I use examples used in class that are based on real data from published scientific literature from several disciplines. I may ask students to engage in conversations with their peers before selecting their answers using i>clickers. Being in interdisciplinary research teams made me a strong believer in collaborative learning and enabled me to publish about aspects of health that involve areas outside my expertise, like single nucleotide polymorphism and genotyping, and the role of families on attenuating depressive symptoms. My collaboration with other peers from genetics to psychology allowed me to go beyond my formal training to explore important questions, and I encourage students to do the same type of collaborative questioning. What do the numbers mean? Are there any differences by gender, race, or age? How some of these variables are associated? Just as I am able to answer such questions only through interdisciplinary research, so too students see how useful it is to share perspectives and methods when trying to make sense of numbers that link behaviors and conditions to specific health consequences. Given their individual interests, students tend to come to different conclusions about the same health problem, and this allows them to see the value of collaboration.

Last but not least, I encourage students to see how statistics can be flawed, and this is key to appreciating the power of statistics. In one exercise, I present students with real-world examples of poor or misleading graphs, or statistics presented in a biased way. Teams of students come up with different solutions to "fix" flawed graphs. Sometimes all it takes is to change the scale on the x- or y-axis, but other times much more work is involved. With this kind of exercise, students become critical thinkers about information presented to them, particularly by the news media.

I draw on my own research interests and practices in class but, conversely, teaching feeds back into my research, as well. As students learn about my research, they ask if they can collaborate with me, which is gratifying to me both as an educator and a researcher. I use every opportunity in my Health Statistics class to start mentoring them. I have mentored several undergraduate students who started with me in that class and then moved to collaborations as part of independent research projects. When I mentor undergraduate students, I endeavor to expose them to all stages of the research process, from data entry to manuscript writing. Students often start by assisting in data entry, questionnaire development, or codebook development in one of my projects. After acquiring an understanding of how data are generated and how it can be used to generate knowledge, they begin to evaluate relevant literature based on available data and their interests. They quickly realize just exactly how the knowledge and expertise in statistics they acquired in Health Statistics class move them from mere number crunchers to active problem solvers. The story of Jilber (Jay) Jerman is a case in point.

Jay was a very fit student who became curious about how aware people his age were about their bodies. Our initial work was to explore the agreement between perceived (self-reported) and actual (measured) body mass index categories in a sample of Mexican college applicants aged eighteen to twenty years. We found that under two-thirds (63.1 percent) accurately reported their weight status categories, and the remaining either overestimated or underestimated their body weight status. We were intrigued by why some students were aware of their body sizes, but others not. To answer these questions, we invited my interdisciplinary collaborators on campus to explore the demographic, behavioral, and psychological correlates of accurate reporting. After many semesters of collaboration, we were gratified to see our final work published in the *Body Image: An International Journal of Research* (Andrade et al., 2012) and received considerable media attention. It was Jay's curiosity that moved me in this direction. Even though much of my work has been focused on the impact of obesity on life expectancy and quality of life, this was the first time I explored the misperceptions about weight and their health consequences, and it would not have been possible without Jay and his experience in the Health Statistics class.

It is Wednesday in May, 9:50 A.M. It is warmer now, and the sun shines outside. As students leave the room for their next class, I am smiling: they have tamed their fears and learned that even though the mathematical equation may seem lifeless, statistics is actually part of their lives. They know how to use and interpret it, which can help them make better decisions that will allow them to live longer and better lives. This can be seen at the end of the semester when they provide me with feedback on the course, as expressed here by one student:

> Whether people are cognizant of it or not, they are constantly bombarded by statistics and mathematics in their day to day lives. In today's world, we are faced with situations on a daily basis where statistics can be applied. Statistics can be used to better examine phenomenon on a deeper level and determine the potential outcome of thousands of events that the human mind alone would not be able to.

They have accomplished so much, and I hope this knowledge will carry them to new adventures on their lives. As they reflect on how this course may be important to their future, I see how empowered they feel.

I am sure I will be using statistics as proof that what I am saying has value.

As a professor, I am thrilled as they improve their understanding of statistics, learn how to make smart decisions in daily life, and learn how to pursue scientific knowledge. It is rewarding to see at the end of the semester how their learned skills enable students to be familiarized with statistics and how they can make use of scientific literature, which can be intimidating.

> Being aware of all the statistics around me was an interesting experience. It is neat to realize how many things we are able to predict and analyze about the world around us.

> The main thing I look for now when I'm reading a research article is a statistic that supports the evidence, but not until taking this course was I able to fully understand its relevance.

As both a researcher and a teacher, I feel privileged to be able to work with a diverse group of students every week and being able to explore new venues of research as I collaborate with some of them. They help me achieve the ultimate goal of my research, which is to understand not only how we can live longer lives, but how we can live better ones.

REFERENCES

Andrade, F. C. D., A. I. N. M. Nazan, M. L. Lebrão, and Y. A. O. Duarte. 2013. "Impact of Obesity and Weight Changes on Disability and Mortality in Brazilian Older Adults." *Journal of Aging and Research*. Article ID: 905094, doi:10.1155/2013/905094.

Andrade, F. C., M. Raffaelli, M. Teran-Garcia, J. A. Jerman, C. A. Garcia; Up Amigos 2009 Study Group. 2012. "Weight-Status Misperception among Mexican Young Adults." *Body Image* 9, no. 1 (2012 Jan): 184–88. doi: 10.1016/j.bodyim.2011.10.006. Epub 2011 Nov 21.

Bruff, Derek. 2009. *Teaching with Classroom Response Systems: Creating Active Learning Environments*. San Francisco: Jossey-Bass. See also http://iclicker.illinois.edu/.

Monteiro, C. A., W. L. Conde, and B. M. Popkin. 2007. "Income-Specific Trends in Obesity in Brazil: 1975–2003." *American Journal of Public Health* 97 (10): 1808–12.

National Center for Health Statistics. 2012. *Health, United States, 2011: With Special Feature on Socioeconomic Status and Health*. Hyattsville, Md. Available at http://www.cdc.gov/nchs/data/hus/hus11.pdf, accessed December 10, 2013.

THE HUMANITY OF TEACHING
Reflections from the Education Justice Project

D. Fairchild Ruggles

Department of Landscape Architecture

with Hugh Bishop, Rebecca Ginsburg, Audrey Petty,
Anke Pinkert, and Agniezska Tuszynska

Since 2008, small groups of volunteers from the University of Illinois at Urbana-Champaign (UIUC) have shuttled out to the Danville Correctional Center, a medium-high-security state prison forty miles away. Friday nights, we enter the drab DCC waiting room with our folders of papers—no DVDs, books, iPods, or cell phones are permitted. Signing the logbook and picking up our IDs at the first guard station, we pass through multiple sets of locked doors, a metal detector, and into the "port" with its heavy sliding gates overlooked by the second guard station, where hanging on the wall are key rings and a locked gun rack. Eventually we enter the prison yard, where uniformed inmates, directed by guards, are walking in double lines to the cafeteria, the gym, or—as we are doing—to the educational building. Some of the guys wave and greet us by name. We know them. They are our students.

We teach in the University of Illinois's Education Justice Project (EJP), which offers four for-credit classes each semester, supported by extracurricular writing and science workshops, a series of guest speakers from UIUC (including Pulitzer Prize–winner Leon Dash and Nobel Peace Prize–winner Don Wuebbels), tutoring sessions, reading groups, and a supplementary program teaching English to inmates whose language is insufficient for them to function in the prison or in society. But more than this, EJP's mission, reflecting the mission of education itself, is to encourage the development of people committed to a thoughtful process that is reflective rather than reactive. Using our research to teach at the prison means furthering that goal with a group of incarcerated men who are not only highly committed to it but also aware of what the world looks like in its absence.

FIGURE 1. The Danville Correctional Center, Illinois. Photograph by Rebecca Ginsburg.

EJP currently serves over 120 incarcerated students and involves almost seventy university faculty, graduate students, staff, and community members in delivering these programs, all on a volunteer basis. We are driven to give our time and seek ways of bringing our research to the prison environment because of what we know about this moment in our society. National and state incarceration rates have never been higher, and the rising numbers have serious consequences for the incarcerated, their families, and all Illinois residents, who pay the fiscal and social costs of maintaining a correctional system that is bursting at the seams. Poverty, lack of educational access, and incarceration are inextricably linked, and the lack of access to higher education among America's poor and within its prisons contributes to high rates of incarceration and recidivism. We provide university education for the students at Danville, yet the impact is felt as far away as Chicago, where many of the inmates come from. For the university and the state, we believe that teaching in EJP models the most crucial function of a public, land-grant research university: to keep discovering meaningful ways of making the research and resources produced by faculty in the humanities, social sciences, and sciences accessible, relevant, beneficial, and even transformative to society broadly conceived.

The experience of teaching behind bars—without a scholarly library, the internet, or an efficient means of communication between teachers and students outside of class time, and facing students whose eagerness

FIGURE 2. The prison yard through which students and instructors walk to reach the Recreation and Education Building. Photograph by Rebecca Ginsburg.

for education and intellectual thought completely outpaces the skills and resources at their disposal, in short, dealing with all kinds of lack all the time—has ironically made us into more effective, thoughtful, and committed teachers. Of necessity, we have adapted and grown flexible as the very limits imposed have caused us to shift attention from the mechanisms of teaching to the humanity of it. EJP draws its extraordinary instructors from all ranks of the university, from graduate students to staff and full professors, whose collaboration is knitted in intense conversations as we carpool to and from Danville, and some of whose threads appear here.

*   *   *

Writer, poet, and professor Audrey Petty, who taught a writing class for EJP in 2012, recalls her first visit to the prison program to observe and decide whether she wanted to teach there: "The presentations that night were complex and interesting, and the conversation that ensued was absolutely lively. Every student seemed to have a stake in what was transpiring in that classroom. In addition to speaking out on the subjects at hand, they listened deeply to one another and, as a result, created an incredible dialogue."

The EJP students do love to talk, as Agniezska Tuszynska—fellow teacher and doctoral candidate in English—discovered in her American fiction course. "At the end of the semester I asked: 'What have you learned from this class?' After giving me *their* answers, the students turned and asked: 'What have *you* learned?' Unprepared, I gave them the best answer I could muster at the moment: 'I became excited about what I do as a teacher and a student.' But I should have told them that, thanks to them, I'd remembered that which the stress and pressure of dissertation writing and looking for a job have caused me partially to forget: that the study of literature *matters* and that it is *thrilling*.

"Recent years have seen the jeopardized status of the humanities within the increasingly profit-oriented system of higher education. In humanities departments, we brace against budget cuts and find it necessary to defend the relevance of what we do. But my involvement with EJP and especially the class I taught there have given me a new level of confidence as a humanities scholar and teacher. I have seen the study of literature, culture, and history bring the best intellectual and spiritual qualities out of a group of students in an environment many would consider actively hostile to the human spirit. In a place where daily life is dehumanizing, I have seen rigorous and meticulous critical analysis lead not just to insightful conclusions but to conclusions based on compassion and empathy for the human condition of others.

"For example, we read Nelson Algren's *Never Come Morning* (1942), a novel about urban violence and street life. Featuring a male protagonist, the story—I thought—was likely to stir my students' identification with the tough existence that it depicted. What I did not expect was that our discussion would focus largely on the struggles of the story's *female* character and the social conditions that women faced during the Great Depression. I did not foresee that within the hyper-masculine culture of the prison, the students would introduce relevant and deeply stirring personal narratives in which they compared the women in their own neighborhoods to the novel's struggling female character. While I had anticipated that the students would identify with the novel, I didn't imagine I would witness them engaging in a feminist analysis.

"This is how I know the humanities matter. Through the critical study of the human condition we discover what we have in common with one another despite our differences. The humanities invite us to confront our prejudices and to interrogate them."

German studies professor Anke Pinkert has volunteered in the EJP program as instructor and workshop organizer for the past three years, an engagement that has fed back into a seminar on film portrayals of incarceration that she now teaches on campus. In 2010, she taught an EJP course based on her research on the Holocaust in film, and she reflected on the experience as follows.

"Similar to mature undergraduates on campus, the men at Danville are passionate, deeply caring, and intellectually ambitious students. They demand the best from their teachers and in turn they give the best of themselves. Grappling with the Holocaust—especially within the prison context—was no easy task, as the Danville students were asked to address difficult questions that often hit close to home. For example: What made it possible for people to marginalize, exclude, incarcerate and finally annihilate their fellow citizens? Or, inversely, how to make sense of one's own acts of perpetration, often related to peer pressure, precarious notions of masculinity, and persistent indoctrination? The starting point for our critical analysis was to practice attentive listening—to the texts and to each other. Sometimes, especially at the beginning of the semester, students clung to entrenched views. But, more often and increasingly, an electric stillness pervaded the classroom, an awareness and receptivity that come from engaging with questions that deeply matter to all of us. One student in the class, explaining how Holocaust education can be transformative, wrote that it had helped him 'to value other people's point of view and to put [himself] in the position of another.'

"It is this kind of purposeful and reciprocal pedagogy, an integrative approach to learning that engages our minds, our hearts, and our souls, that I bring back to our traditional campus. Teaching at Danville inspires me to practice education and research that combines intellectual rigor with thoughtfulness, analysis, and feeling. This also requires that we put ourselves as teachers and students into the histories we study, that we deeply connect what we teach to ourselves. For example, I now teach a discovery course for freshmen on campus about mass imprisonment in the U.S. and the ways the media and movies shape our understanding of 'incarceration at a distance.' Through critical dialogue and self-reflections, students often begin to recognize their own fascination with a culture that turns imprisonment into a spectacle.

"Higher education can and needs to be a site for hope and renewal. If we can find the courage to view our society holistically, that is if we begin to be more deliberate in our awareness that we are all interconnected, then mutual accountability—the collective responsibility to care and to take care of one another—will become inevitable. Teaching for EJP has taught me that we as a university have the privilege and the obligation to be a central part of this transformative vision."

Many of the people who teach for EJP have been astonished by their experiences in the nontraditional classrooms there. We knew we were doing something good for the men at the prison, with beneficial repercussions for the communities they come from and society as a whole. But many of us, like language and linguistics instructor Hugh Bishop, did not realize how humanizing and indeed how pleasurable EJP would be. "Prisons are popularly thought to be places that should borrow a sign from Dante for their main gates: 'Abandon hope all ye who enter here.' Media coverage usually emphasizes the negative, and publications abound relating to the violence and general nastiness of penitentiaries. The inevitable effect is a thoroughly depressing picture of penal institutions in the U.S. in the 21st century. So, no surprise that when I approached my first visit to the prison a few years ago, I was feeling considerable trepidation."

But he confessed, "I expected the worst, yet experienced the best. My initial impressions were very different from what I had imagined and dreaded, and those positive impressions have now been reinforced by actual experience. To quote from Milton's *Paradise Lost*: 'The mind is its own place, and in itself / Can make a Heaven of Hell, a Hell of Heaven.' In an often toxic environment, our EJP students are firmly in the 'make a Heaven of Hell' camp. The EJP Language Partners program, which I supervise, illustrates this.

"The idea for a Language Partners program originated with a student inmate. The original plan was that bilingual inmates in EJP would help Spanish-speaking ones in the general prison population learn enough English to be able to take adult educational and vocational classes, and to be able to function better in the daily activities of a prison run in English. The language tutoring program has grown and evolved to include ESL [English as a Second Language] teacher training, and yet, certain characteristics remain stable. In the last place you might expect it, our students are becoming ever more caring, creative, sensitive, and committed to the process of education, often sacrificing their limited and valuable recreation time, to help others.

"This is why EJP has been so successful: because in a wasteland it provides an oasis offering mutual respect for all. It offers myriad educational opportunities and sets the highest standards. It demonstrates potential for personal transformation and then demands it. Importantly, it relinquishes much of the ownership of the program to the participants, and because it is truly theirs, it is valued accordingly. Having chosen to educate (they might say 'liberate') themselves through the University of Illinois's facilitation, the consequence for the men at Danville is growing manifestations of initiative, self-respect, autonomy, and growing pedagogical competence.

"Lest the attitude of the EJP instructors seem delusional, let me say that I know we work with an elite group of student prisoners whom we see in a very restricted context, and I know that many of those in the prison have been found guilty of heinous offences. Nonetheless, my abiding impression is one of warmth and humanity. There's a paradox for you."

It's worth noting about the comments above that it was a student who first had the Language Partners idea—evidence of the contagious enthusiasm faculty can generate when they move their research passions into classrooms of all kinds. In fact, the instructors' commitment to the Education Justice Project is routinely responded to in kind by the students. In an EJP newsletter column, EJP student T. Ray X wrote: "I smile when listening to my classmates discuss a book we all thought we'd hate but found we really enjoyed. All the challenges I face in prison and in life, I address them through my education. Learning is my 'yes, I can;' it's the 'change I can believe in . . . ' Even when no one else believes in me. Education, higher learning, knowledge will set me free."

Why does teaching in the prison have such an effect on teachers? Rebecca Ginsburg, EJP's founder and director, mused: "I think that what we see at Danville is what happens when exceptional students meet exceptional teachers. The instructors who self-select to teach at the prison are dedicated, reflective, serious, and skilled, and yet teaching on campus, they don't regularly experience the sparkle that characterizes their EJP classes.

FIGURE 3. Education Justice Project students in one of the UIUC study rooms at the Danville Correctional Center. The students are (*left to right*): Joseph Bigsby, George Bledsoe, Johnny Page, Kemuyah ben Rakemeyahu, and Spankey (Kenneth) Davis. Photograph by Rebecca Ginsburg.

The difference is the students, men who have already sacrificed much to pursue their education and have already witnessed what a difference it makes in their lives, so that by the time we meet them, they're committed. There's very little cynicism among EJP students. They don't ask 'will this be on the test?' or 'what's the point of this exercise?' They get it, and they trust us as teachers. As a group, they're mature, with plenty of real-life experience. Thoughtful and dedicated. Respectful of one another and their instructors. Smart enough to have gotten through tough schooling conditions in the prison."

These accounts may suggest that the Education Justice Project primarily affects a select group of men at the Danville state prison, but it extends much further. EJP regularly hosts family days in Chicago, and at those events, it is deeply moving for us to be able to praise the accomplishments of a man, imprisoned for the past fifteen years, to his mother and grandmother, and even perhaps his children, who have not forgotten him and remain hopeful that he will return to them to lead a meaningful life. The long distance from Chicago to Danville impedes visiting, yet the families find surprising ways of staying connected, mailing books and photocopies, and even reaching into their pockets—hardly full to begin with—to donate money to EJP. Because of its reach beyond the prison walls, EJP's impact is both wide and deep. The children and siblings of many Danville students are taking college classes because their fathers and brothers set the example for them. For EJP students, to be able to positively guide youth in this way, even while incarcerated, is a source of enormous pride. When research and teaching can accomplish this in even a small way, it is arguably a powerful combination for social good.

In *Cultivating Humanity* (1997), the philosopher Martha Nussbaum advocates that "we recognize the worth of human life wherever it occurs and see ourselves as bound by common human abilities and problems to people who lie at a great distance from us." She elaborates three capacities essential to the cultivation of humanity. First is "the capacity for critical examination of oneself and one's traditions." Second is the recognition that we are not just citizens of a community but "human beings bound to all other human beings by ties of recognition and concern." Finally, she proposes that we expand beyond simply collecting facts and information about the world, and extend our reach into what she calls, "the narrative imagination." That imagination is the ability to walk a mile in another person's shoes, to have empathy. In its embrace and teaching of these principles within the harsh environment of a state prison, the Education Justice Project is truly visionary.

Great though the impact has been on the lives of EJP students, the lives of the teachers have been equally affected. We are enriched by the experience of being present to observe and encourage profound transformative growth in our students. They do not ask for an easy break. They simply want the opportunity to excel. It never fails to amaze us that the single greatest gift we can give them is to expect the best of them.

NOTE

The Education Justice Project's website is http://www.educationjustice.net/home/.

PRAIRIE TALES
The Life of the Lecture at Illinois

Laurie Johnson
Department of Germanic Languages and Literatures

I have been teaching fairy tales since shortly after I arrived at the University of Illinois about eleven years ago, when I was assigned a course that reliably brings high numbers of students into the relatively small Department of Germanic Languages and Literatures: The Grimms' Fairy Tales in Their European Context. My research field is romanticism, but the nineteenth century was the only thing that tied me to the Grimm brothers' oddly progressive *and* regressive project of collecting folklore from all over Europe and repackaging it as "German." I knew nothing about folklore studies, and hadn't seen the Disney remakes of the canonical tales. In addition, I seriously doubted that a class on fairy tales could be rigorous enough to satisfy the college's Advanced Composition and Western Culture requirements—and I was jadedly sure that the large enrollments had to do with the fact that these requirements could be satisfied by, well, reading "Snow White." Finally, I had no experience teaching large lecture courses, and while I knew that "service" courses like Grimms' Fairy Tales were necessary for my unit to thrive, I was sure I was not the right person for the task. But my prairie tale has a happy ending, indeed. The methods of rigorous analysis that I've taught my students to apply to fairy tales are the same methods that now guide one of my current research projects—a book on new psychoanalytic approaches to fairy tales.

One of the first and most difficult tales I ask students to consider is "The Juniper Tree," a fairy tale published by the Brothers Grimm and highly popular in the nineteenth century. It includes decapitation, cannibalism, metamorphosis, fiery resurrection, and a murder committed by a bird that crushes a wicked stepmother with a huge millstone. Despite all the talk about how today's young people are inured to violence, students are unfailingly shocked by "Tree" and its tragicomic vision of a family's personal apocalypse and questionable redemption. But after they recover from their initial astonishment, the students notice some strange things about the tale in addition to its violent content. The story opens not with the standard "Once upon a time" but rather with semi-specific dating: "Long, long ago, some two thousand years or so . . ." At the moment when the villainess murders her stepson, "the devil possess(es) her," which some students understand as a kind of exculpation. The heroic, kind father enjoys eating his own son for dinner, exclaiming about the grisly stew: "I feel as if it were all mine." These anomalies and surprises, together with the story's shocking substance, direct students' attention to the dense texture of the text, encouraging and demanding close reading as well as in-depth discussion.

Although it is set just before the birth of Jesus of Nazareth, "The Juniper Tree" ends up taking our class directly to a set of issues crucial to Western culture around 1800, right to the vexed nexus of the Enlightenment and romanticism. And this is what the course is fundamentally about: reading well- and lesser-known fairy tales, radical fictions, narrowly and closely in order to understand the radical facts of history more deeply and broadly. Sustained and patient attention to compact phrases in short texts permits us to think in informed and critical ways about the "big texts" that still surround us: the stories of European history and Western culture, and of how assumptions based on those stories affect how we read and speak today.

In fact, the students and I reflect on the value of humanistic inquiry all the time. One week was devoted to the arguably fundamentalist ideology behind the Grimms' philological project, and students made responsible and thoughtful connections to rising fundamentalism (of various kinds) today. Psychoanalysis, a limpid model for acknowledging and thinking through existential crises, is another tool we use in class to grapple with surprisingly difficult concepts in fairy tales. When the Goose Girl's passivity seems mind-boggling, or Brother's self-destructive actions (in "Brother and Sister") incomprehensible, students can envision that same historical nexus of the Enlightenment and romanticism as an externalization of a psychic landscape in which rational and irrational impulses struggle for dominance. A better understanding of the Oedipal complex helps students to see the centrality of loss in the tales—loss of home or loss of a parent marks the beginning of many of these stories—and to understand that while the hero or heroine often compensates for that loss by finding a new home and a new love, the tales themselves are massive compensation strategies for us, for the readers and listeners who must face mortality and who desperately need these simultaneously fantastic and truthful fictions to help us navigate reality.

The emergence, in my classes, of psychoanalysis as a robust model for understanding tales has linked my own research agenda to my teaching. I have begun editing the aforementioned volume of essays on psychoanalytic approaches to tales, tentatively titled "Freud and the Fairy Tale: New Approaches to Very Old Stories." Without the "service" course, I would never be making this research leap. My own interests have been most productively displaced, and the "service" done has also been to my own benefit.

I am sure that the course's form is crucial to the exciting feedback loop I am experiencing between my own research and teaching, and that this type of loop is being created in numerous other lecture classrooms across campus. The close readings that the students and I perform of "The Juniper Tree" and many other texts all happen in a planned, yet ultimately unpredictable and dynamic, forum: the space and time of the lecture. I have become convinced that there is a strong and necessary place for the humanistic lecture course at the University of Illinois, even as our ways of teaching and knowledge production inevitably change. My eleven-plus years of experience with the lecture course format and its enormous productivity for my unit and for my own work have helped persuade me. The style and scope of the lecture course have allowed me to combine new knowledge (in my case, about fairy tales and folklore studies) with my previous research in romanticism studies and psychoanalysis. I would not have done any of this, in turn, without the close reading work accomplished by my students over the years. The lecture course's form mirrors its function as an old, yet simultaneously ever-new way of storytelling that matters.

This form is changing dramatically. New technologies and ways of delivering course content implicitly call the classroom lecture into question. Sherry Turkle notes that our preoccupation with social media in particular means we are now "alone together." While I agree that the effects of new media are potentially isolating, I recognize that such media may also offer new ways to advance the dynamic communications among teachers and groups of students that have made lecture classrooms so essential at the University of Illinois. Recent concerns about the loss of real-time interaction between teacher and student subscribe in part to an overly black-and-white distinction between "reality" and "virtuality." Debates about the impact of new technologies on lecture teaching were also common among scholars who were the Grimm brothers' contemporaries. The lecture as it emerged in Germany around 1800, for instance, already had a "hypermedial" quality, combining the use of new print technologies with an insistence on interactive discussion.

The classroom lecture as it exists in the United States today is indebted to the lecture at the German university around 1800. At the beginning of the nineteenth century, the future was being contested, in part, at the site of the new research university. Johann Gottlieb Fichte's *Addresses to the German Nation* (1808), his political essays beginning in the 1790s, and Wilhelm von Humboldt's *Theory of Human Education* (1793), among other texts of that time, helped construct a vision of pedagogy as simultaneously beholden to ancient ideals of learning and to a modern view of the university. German Idealists wished to uphold the ancient model of knowledge production as happening best during discussion between teacher and student, but they also wanted their universities to reflect the fruits of the Enlightenment, including the fact that increasing numbers of people were reading and were able to own books. The lecture as conceived by Fichte and Humboldt was interactive and employed various media at what Sean Franzel has called "the nexus of print and oral publication" around 1800, a time in which "scholars lectured with one eye on the lecture hall and one on the print public sphere, aggressively pursuing attention through all media at their disposal." Humboldt in particular envisioned the individual and his education as utterly dependent on his ability to exist in a community of learners, and this is consistent with his view of language as constructive; for example, language creates knowledge dynamically, rather than only representing it statically.

The Grimms' "Juniper Tree" is hypermedial, too, as it unites references to various cultural traditions and texts (including Ovid's *Metamorphoses*, the Old Testament, and older fairy tales) in a narrative pastiche that includes fragments of poetry, dialogue, and third-person narration. Students invariably make more sense out of this hybrid tale when discussing it together. At the conclusion of "Tree," brother, sister, and father are reunited in a scene simultaneously Oedipal and communal. The reunion between father and son (or, between knowledge and the knower) is enabled and mediated by the sister (or, by community, by that which gives life). When the students and I discuss this tale, and I lecture on the traditions behind it and the histories that inform it, we "reunite" in the present classroom as well as "resurrect" the text and its pasts. In a sense, we reunite in the "home" of the university, through the blending of writing and discussion. Could we do this online? Perhaps. But I would argue that there should be a place for presence, as well, for the rich presence of this text, and for mediating research about it in real time. In the lecture, writing (absence) and speech (presence) reunite. Research and teaching come together as well, as in the lecture-discussion my work outside the classroom comes inside—comes home. The lecture is, in short, one kind of model for life.

My lectures today are "hypermedial," as were those around 1800, but now with the integration of images and film enabled by classroom technologies.

My argument here for "presence" is not based on venerating the authority of the professor or on valorizing the spoken word over the written, or flesh-and-blood presence over the screen. The dynamic learning communities that continually remake meaning in and out of all kinds of tales remind us that the interactive lecture classroom is a place for delivering and producing knowledge, and thus that the lecture connects us to one another: it connects students to instructor, students to the world of the humanities and thus also to the universe of the university, and students to Europe and other cultures. The modern lecture brings the past into the present without insisting that the present must obey the past. The lecture is a condensation of life, and it is one answer to our ongoing need, not to be "alone together," but to read, speak, and be together.

BIBLIOGRAPHY

Bettelheim, Bruno. *The Uses of Enchantment: The Meaning and Importance of Fairy Tales.* New York: Vintage, 2010.

Franzel, Sean. "The Romantic Lecture in an Age of Paper (Money): Jean Paul's Literary Aesthetics across Print and Orality." *RaVoN (Romanticism and Victorianism on the Net)* 57–58 (February–May 2010). http://id.erudit.org/iderudit/1006516ar.

Freud, Sigmund. *Civilization and Its Discontents.* Translated by James Strachey. New York: W. W. Norton, 2005.

Grimm, Jacob, and Wilhelm Grimm. *The Complete Fairy Tales of the Brothers Grimm.* Translated by Jack Zipes. New York: Bantam, 2003.

Hohendahl, Peter Uwe. "Humboldt Revisited: Liberal Education, University Reform, and Opposition to the Neoliberal University." *New German Critique* 38.2 (2011): 159–96.

Humboldt, Wilhelm von. *Theorie der Bildung des Menschen* (1793; *Theory of Human Education*). Vols. 1 and 2, *Gesammelte Schriften.* Berlin: Akademie der Wissenschaften, 1903–36.

James, David. "Fichte on the Vocation of the Scholar and the (Mis)use of History." *Review of Metaphysics* 63.3 (2010): 539–66.

Tatar, Maria. *The Annotated Brothers Grimm.* London: W. W. Norton, 2004.

———. *The Hard Facts of the Grimms' Fairy Tales.* Princeton, N.J.: Princeton University Press, 2003.

Turkle, Sherry. *Alone Together: Why We Expect More from Technology and Less from Each Other.* New York: Basic Books, 2011.

Engineering Professors Who Are Reengineering Their Courses
The iFoundry Perspective

Luisa-Maria Rosu
I-STEM, College of Engineering

with Betty Jo Barrett, Bryan Wilcox, Geoffrey Herman,
Raymond Price, and Lizanne DeStefano

The University of Illinois has a well-deserved reputation for rigor in engineering education, with instructional content heavily oriented toward mathematics and science. Faculty members in the Illinois Foundry for Innovation in Engineering Education (iFoundry) have been redesigning their courses by using instructional contexts that allow students to see meaningful relationships between abstract ideas and practical applications. I met biweekly with a group of these faculty members as they examined how the new course designs generate challenges and encourage departures from traditional engineering teaching. The group included Ray Price, Brian Wilcox, Geoffrey Herman, and Betty Barrett. As the discussions and course designs developed, I observed that each instructor transformed his or her teaching by applying principles from their particular disciplines and by using the experience of their own research. They modeled, in other words, the very kind of feedback loop that faculty in this collection are addressing by asking students to reflect on their own passions, processes, and methods as a core part of their problem-solving projects.

"How does it happen," asks Bryan Wilcox, the instructor of an elective course on project design, "that, for very similar project situations, both senior and first-year students struggle with same issue? After I probe with questions, the freshman is able to locate the physics principle and proceed measuring only the needed variable; the senior continues the trial and error process." An experienced engineer who had worked at General Electric, Northrup Grumman, and John Deere, Bryan Wilcox has long been interested in how professionals collaborate to carry out their projects. His engineering research has affected his teaching by making him want to involve introductory level students in complicated, real projects from the start. This helps students recognize the knowledge and skills they will need to solve a problem, while enhancing their motivation.

"I am primarily involved," says Wilcox, "in programs where I teach within the context of engineering projects. Executing work in the framework of a project more accurately reflects the nature of work our students will face once they are practicing engineers. Learning the skills best gathered through experience is a key element of structuring work in this manner. I am very positive about using projects as a framework for learning and feel my experience has revealed some fundamental realities of human nature when attempting to learn abstract principles in the context of real problems."

What's unusual about Wilcox's courses is that students must identify the problem their project will solve. This differs from more traditional project-based engineering courses in which the professor assigns the problem. As Wilcox explains, this departure from the norm enhances the students' motivation.

> This simple twist of letting them work on topics they care about has profound implications for the depth of learning and amount of effort they are willing to apply. When I set about creating the course structure for IEFX Projects, I was primarily concerned with getting freshmen excited by and involved in real engineering work as soon as possible. Although they lack coursework and knowledge of the more complicated techniques, they can still apply themselves well with the knowledge they already have.
>
> With a little cleverness, I have found that every project attempted by students has provided significant learning opportunities in real, rigorous engineering subjects: structural mechanics, fluids, circuit theory, etc. I only need to keep in tune with the teams, and recognize these teaching moments and bring them out. I have unlocked students' real interest and enthusiasm in tackling and learning these subjects and principles. The students are energetic and engaged to learn the material because it has context and is relevant to something they are interested in.

As Wilcox explains, focusing the students on their own design projects encourages them to hone skills that are often taught in higher level engineering courses.

> Freshmen with no prior programming experience created functioning mobile apps that solve real problems experienced by them or others. Other freshmen created complicated, Web-enabled, mechatronic systems that can dispense pills on a schedule remotely directed by a doctor. Others built autonomous vehicles that incorporate sophisticated control schemes to eliminate errors

and oscillations in the resulting systems. These projects require skills typically taught in upper-level classes. In this context, the students recognized the need to acquire the skills, find the resources, learn the material, and apply it to solve their problems.

A survey of Professor Wilcox's students indicated that they thought communication skills were the skills most essential to the success of their group projects. When I asked Wilcox to comment on this, he compared the experiences of his students with those of real-world engineers. "How do we develop the capacity to make engineering decisions based on limited and incomplete information? What really matters in a problem is how we structure information so that our predictive theories can be put to use and applied," he responded. "The learning experiences of these students taught me about different ways how to develop a 'feel' for proper direction when faced with overwhelming amounts of information, learning what are reasonable assumptions when tackling problems and how those assumptions can be verified. These are all part of communication in any group work."

Geoffrey Herman is another faculty member involved in the iFoundry project. He applies to his teaching some of the skills he uses in his engineering research: analysis, and forming theories or hypotheses he can test. And he observes that when students have more freedom, he can understand more about their learning needs. In fall 2011, he taught the experimental section of a sophomore course in electrical and computer engineering. He also supervised discussion-section activities. "I design my classroom to give students learning choices, both active and passive, that help them discover their personal passions for learning and for the topic as well as connect them with other students who share their passions. Self-Determination Theory claims that we can promote students' motivation by giving them senses of autonomy, competence, relatedness, and purpose."

One of the challenges of teaching courses that focus on students' interests and choices is providing appropriate guidance when students need it. As Herman explains, "You know, giving students this type of freedom has surprisingly given me a better understanding of the engineering topics that I teach and a greater clarity about what my students need to know to be successful in engineering. I have learned that instructors can also thrive when given the autonomy and support to redesign their classrooms to promote students' learning." Herman believes the course has "created a synergy that allows me to immerse myself in learning and helping students. My research informs my teaching by giving me theoretical frameworks and analysis skills to better understand my classroom. Conversely, my teaching gives me a living laboratory in which I can test the emerging theories and hypotheses of my research."

A faculty member in the School of Labor and Employment Relations, Betty Barrett examines the balance between participation and autonomy in her research about sociotechnical systems. She also observes this balance in her classroom. "Teaching a class titled Leading Sustainable Change could provoke deep personal reflection," Barrett says as she explains why she agreed to teach the course.

> I wondered whether I would model leadership appropriately and whether the students would experience change through their efforts in the class. In my mind, there are three key elements to this accomplishment; trust, autonomy, and mutual responsibility or purpose. Participation and autonomy are the links that most clearly connect my teaching style with my research. I study sociotechnical systems as devised by Emery and Trist in the early to mid-twentieth century. These scholars believed that the introduction of technology would necessitate increased participation of the workers and would only work when the levels of worker autonomy was heightened. I see this as a direct link to student directed education. Students can take advantage of technology to facilitate their own intellectual growth and take charge of their own learning. My teaching job would be to create the space within which this happens.

An important part of this creation is to invite students to understand the rationale for why the course is designed in this way.

> Building and sustaining trust is essential for the relationship that I developed with the students. I had to be frank, consistent, and willing to give the students the autonomy to make their own choices. We discussed why the readings were selected and what I hoped they would learn. This meant that they could question me and my choices and that I had to respond respectfully to these exchanges. On the other hand, they came to class prepared for the discussion because that was their responsibility to themselves, me, and the other students.

After observing several of her class meetings, I noticed that Professor Barrett encourages students to talk about how to organize their projects when they had not yet identified a problem, much less the change they were supposed to attain. When I asked her about this, Barrett explained, "Forces such as competition and innovation drive the global dynamics that shape our society. Students become the workers who create our world. They will need skills that allow them to be self-managed as well as team–based workers. I believe that these skills need to be practiced so that students become comfortable taking on this responsibility. In this environment, I learned to reinvent my role as an educator as well."

The application of engineering skills to instructional design is a common practice among iFoundry faculty, although the focus on student agency in various aspects of problem solving is a unique payoff, as apparent from each of the experiences discussed here. Wilcox, Herman, and Barrett apply skills gained from their individual engineering research specialties to their teaching. Together they are reengineering students' experiences and opening up new worlds of technical skill and imaginative possibility that will help those students in the world of work that awaits them.

REFERENCES

Cronbach, Lee J. 1963. "Course Improvement through Evaluation." *Teachers College Record* 64: 672–83.

Graham, R. 2012. "Achieving Excellence in Engineering Education: The Ingredients of Successful Change." London: Royal Academy of Engineering. www.raeng.org.uk/change.

Herman, G., L. M. Rosu, and K. Trenshaw. 2012. "Empowering Teaching Assistants to Become Agents of Education Reform." Frontiers in Education Conference, Seattle, Wash., October.

It's More than a "Ghetto Story"
Using Dancehall as a Pedagogical Tool in the Classroom

Karen Flynn
Departments of Gender and Women's Studies,
and African American Studies

I teach Black Women in the Diaspora, a course where, similar to my own research on Black Canadian women, there is a paucity of sources. Thus, I apply
the same principles in my teaching that I use for my research. Coupled with
scholarly analysis, I "creatively reconstruct histories of Black women from
available fragments of sources" (Flynn 2008, 445) to write a narrative about
their experiences beginning with their childhoods, migratory movements,
and professional work lives as well as unpaid and volunteer work. Equally
significant, I pay special attention to human agency and Black women as
social actors—not merely victims—in their own right. Thus, throughout my
book, *Moving beyond Borders: Black Canadian and Caribbean Women in
the Diaspora* (2011), I demonstrate how my subjects made conscious decisions about their lives, regardless of the oppression they encountered. My
goal is to provide a more holistic account of Black women's lives in both
my research and teaching.

The methods I use in the class are critical to addressing the course objectives: understanding how Black women's lives are intimately connected
despite geographic location and how historical/structural/institutional forces
play a role in how they are situated across various locales. To that end, I
model for students three useful methods—a relatable site or context; documentary evidence; and dancehall (a derivative of reggae) lyrics—to help
students think about the specificity of Black women and girls' lived experiences. By the end of the course, students have developed a more complex
portrait of Black women than is possible by looking mainly at the negative
images available in reality TV, popular media, and music.

To devote an entire semester to a group of women who are often ignored, marginalized, and misrepresented makes this intellectual initiative both challenging and exciting. Consequently, a major challenge I have faced in teaching a course solely about Black women is the reconciliation of their seeming invisibility despite their presence as subjects in class readings and lectures. Whether during class or on the course discussion board, students tend to talk about Black people or women generally. To preserve the emphasis on Black women, I incorporated dancehall and rap music. These popular musical genres are useful in that they enable students to grasp fundamental principles and organize concepts relevant to exploring and analyzing Black women's lives. Of course, I am cognizant of dancehall and rap music's reputation as misogynistic, violent, and homophobic, but, to quote Public Enemy, "Don't Believe the Hype."[1] First, neither dancehall nor rap—as with rock music—is solely about misogyny, violence, and queer bashing. And, even if some aspects of dancehall and rap music trouble our commonsense sensibilities, allowing students to critically analyze why this might be the case is part of the educational experience.[2] I, too, engage in a similar analysis when my research subjects behave in ways that deviate from my own societal expectations and norms.

The historical factors that precipitate the movement of Black women across borders are the foci of my research. I compare and contrast the experiences of Black Canadian–born women whose ancestors migrated to Canada from what is now the United States as fugitives, free and manumitted slaves, and Caribbean-born women who migrated directly to Canada or to Britain and then to Canada. Included in the Black Canadian–born cohort are those who migrated to the United States or cross the border daily from Windsor, Ontario, to work in Detroit, Michigan. In class we explore globalization and how, as a process, it has contributed to uneven economies in the Caribbean, resulting in mass migration from the region.

To help students understand the impact of globalization on Jamaica, and by extension the Caribbean region, we watch Stephanie Black's provocative documentary, *Life and Debt*, which explores the impact of the International Monetary Fund (IMF) on the island.[3] Students see the aftermath of colonialism and learn how structural adjustment programs, based on the incentive of transforming a borrower nation into a free-market enterprise, impact Jamaica. Discussions following the documentary, especially if the students are first-years, tend to be superficial. The propensity is to define the United States in particular terms, specifically "developed," and always morally, technologically, and intellectually superior to the citizens of the "Third World." Evident in these discussions is what Chandra Mohanty refers to as "ethnocentric universalism" (1991, 55), which depends on the simplistic binary construct of "us" and "them." From my students' vantage point, globalization and its attendant problems impact only the "Third World." This is the moment that I bring the discussion back to the United States.

Since I have an affinity for Detroit, I feel this is the perfect site to explore the economic, political, and social factors that led to the development of the nation's inner cities. In a short lecture, I begin with the Great Migration (1910–30) from the South, underscoring the fact that migration can be internal to a country as well as external. I focus on Detroit's "glory days," when it was the nation's fastest growing boomtown and home to the highest-paid blue-collar workers. I ask the class the following question: How is it that Detroit now has the highest rates of joblessness, poverty, physical decay, racial isolation and segregation, and crime? At this point, I highlight the historical/structural/institutional forces, such as restrictive covenants (prohibiting the use or occupancy of a house by nonwhite people) and white flight (movement of whites and a few middle-class Blacks) to the suburbs. I explain how globalization (outsourcing and automation) also contributed to Detroit's current crisis. From this exercise, students draw connections in relation to the migratory patterns of African American and Caribbean women at different historical moments. Second, this exercise complicates students' dichotomous views of the "First" and "Third World." They astutely recognize that despite the United States's superior economic, political, and social power, as a nation, it suffers significant cleavages along class and race lines that produce conditions akin to those of the "Third World." The dancehall song and music video "Ghetto Story," a collaboration between Jamaican dancehall artist Baby Cham and R&B singer-songwriter Alicia Keys, serves as illustration in the classroom.

Since Baby Cham's stanzas of "Ghetto Story" are written in Jamaican Creole or Patois, I provide students with the lyrics as we watch the music video and translate whenever possible.[4] (To provide some context for readers: the music video supposedly depicts Baby Cham growing up in one of Kingston's ghettos, but also gives the impression that Keys had a similar experience in the United States. Hence, the music video vacillates between "Cham" and "Keys" singing together as adults recalling their childhood experiences of ghetto life.) We operate then from the premise that the music video is intended to "reflect" to some degree the artists' lives. To my disappointment, the first time we watched "Ghetto Story" in class, students immediately focused on Baby Cham. They didn't really pay attention to Keys or remember her "survival story," and by extension they also missed the structural inequalities that plague Black women and girls in the United

States. Students preferred to look outside of their own nation for blame. This oversight is significant because Keys's voice begins the song: "Here's my, ghetto story (story), been in hell through the fire, now, gonna take it higher. Here is my survival story . . ."[5] I took students' overlooking of "Keys's" narrative to reiterate how Black women and girls are often absent in larger diasporic discussions. That moment was a note to self: "As an instructor, your responsibility is to ensure that "Keys's" narrative" is foregrounded. This meant formulating specific questions to guide the discussion.

I asked students to take notes during the music video and in particular to highlight specific lyrics that addressed the following questions: What, if any, are the commonalities in the "ghetto story" of the "Keys" and Baby Cham characters? How is the "ghetto" space gendered? How is the intersection of race, class, gender, and geographic location reflected in "Ghetto Story"? Are there examples of resistance? After watching the video, we began to answer the questions. Students quickly observed that both "Keys" and Baby Cham as represented in their childhoods live with their mothers. Keys's mother, who is white in real life, is portrayed as white in the video; her racial identity is important given that it is Black sole-supporting mothers living in inner cities who are usually the face of poverty in the U.S. media. Even though Baby Cham mentioned that his mother worked for remuneration, the class assumed the same for "Keys's" mother. Having discussed Black women's labor at length in the class, including my own scholarship on migrant nurses, the students were able to pinpoint how qualifications, education, and training create differential experiences for Black women. In my own work, I insist on recognizing that Black women are not a monolithic group—rather, they are differentiated by additional factors besides those mentioned above, such as time of migration, age, and sexuality.

Students were less confident in explaining how the "ghetto" is gendered because the lyrics do not explicitly address the issue of space. Space is also germane to my own research. I explore identity formation and reformation as it relates to migration, but also how Black bodies transform spaces that are usually the purview of white women, such as nursing. To assist my students, I rephrased the question by asking whether there are differences in how girls and boys experience the "ghetto" as a space to play and live. Here, I am interested in students thinking daily about the material reality of inner-city life. Students noted from the video that both boys and girls are outdoors playing, but less clear to them is how the play itself is gendered, which is where I encouraged them to focus on the play activities "Keys" participates in. They noted that she is playing and laughing with her friends. The space, however, is unclean and unsafe: Keys "remember[s] playing over needles in the street" as well as seeing sex workers and other women "selling their bodies for dope."[6] It is not only the neighborhood that is unsafe.

In the video, as Keys walks to the subway, a homeless man stares at her, her nervousness obvious. Upon her arrival at school, the girl enters the premises when a teacher opens a locked gate, which is reminiscent of a prison. Some of my African American students who live in Chicago's South Side were able to identify with some aspects of Keys's female narrative. One semester, an African American student told the story of visiting a white friend who lived in the suburbs and how surprised she was by the number of trees, the expanses of grass in the neighborhood, and the presence of birds twittering in the morning. On other occasions, my students discussed the preponderance of liquor stores, fast-food chains, predatory lending companies (payday loans), and the absence of Starbucks as stark examples of the difference between the suburbs and inner cities in the United States.

Filmed in Kingston, Baby Cham's narrative in "Ghetto Story" involves activities that students identify as typically male. Instead of attending school, the boy ("go street go roam") hangs out with his friends. There is bullying, retaliation, and ultimately violence between Cham, his friends, and a group of other boys. The violence led to the migration of one of the boy's friends to the United States. My students tend to miss the point that the friend was able to migrate to the United States. At that juncture in the class discussion, I usually clarify any changes that have occurred in the laws regarding migration and misconceptions about migration, the most common being "everybody wants to migrate" to the United States. For example, in the film *Life and Debt*, the narrator explains that North American tourists (mostly white and economically viable) are able to cross borders effortlessly by showing their driver's licenses. Director Stephanie Black notes that for Caribbean peoples to migrate to the countries of the tourists involves a protracted process, which sometimes takes years. They are also not easily welcomed as visitors when they finally arrive, either. By now students will have read my article, "Experience and Identity: Black Immigrant Nurses to Canada, 1950–1980" (2004) providing them with a background to the migration policies in Canada; they know that people do not always migrate for economic reasons.

Resistance and agency is a theme that is germane to my research. For me, it is important that students recognize the various ways people resist oppression even when it is not always obvious, or in some cases, when it is illegal. I point to the latter as one manifestation of globalization and inequality. The most discernible reflection of resistance is embodied in the "Ghetto Story" chorus at the beginning of the song. Both the boy and

the girl ("Keys" and Baby Cham) "made it out of the Ghetto"—they survived—hence "so many reasons to sing now." Depending on the makeup of
the class (African-American juniors and seniors), students are able identify
the expectation of "lifting as we climb"; those who "make it" are expected
to assist others, which is embodied in the following: "We got the kingdom
so we have to make way / And now the whole community can live greatly
. . ." While this form of agency is apparent, I pinpoint the following as
less-explicit examples of resistance, the girl's insistence to be "somebody":
"Big dreams in my head empty my tummy / Might crack a smile but ain't
nothin funny."[7] I emphasize the universality of the ability to dream, which
everyone can relate to. Moreover, students are also expected to identify
the resistive strategy of "making do," "to make something from nothing,"
in order to cushion the family in times of crisis (Khalideen and Khalideen
2002, 108), evident in Keys's recollection that all "we ever ate was white
rice and honey."[8]

Another less-explicit example of resistance is Cham's critique of the Jamaican government. I underscore how reggae and some dancehall music,
like rap music, can be characterized as protest music due to the socially
conscious messages reflected in the lyrics. Cham's lyrics read, "Jamaica gets
screw, tru greed an glutton / Politics manipulate and press yutes button"
(Jamaica is messed up, due to greed and glutton / politics is used as tool of
manipulation, which agitates the youths).[9] Here, Caribbean governments
are also implicated in contributing to the conditions of Caribbean islands.
Still, students are sympathetic to the complex forces (as in the case of the
late Michael Manley, former prime minister of Jamaica), which led to the
signing of the IMF agreement and contribute, whether intentionally or not,
to the current crisis.

As I conducted my research on Black Canadian women, I would often think
of the Jamaican saying "likkle likkle mek nuff nuff" (a little makes a lot).
For me, it means using whatever sources are available to tell the story of
Black women in Canada; I apply the same principle to teaching. Using a
variety of methods helps students see how the lives of Black women and
girls in the United States and the Caribbean are often shaped by similar
economic, political, and social factors. The use of Baby Cham and Alicia
Keys's "Ghetto Story" in particular provides a way for my students to think
about the specificity of Black women and girls' lives across the African
diaspora. Ultimately, the song becomes more than a "ghetto story" as we
underscore relevant themes that are generally eschewed, in order for them

to think more broadly about the intersections of gender, race, class, and nation—subjects that are also critical to my own research.

NOTES

1. This oft-quoted, appropriate phrase is the title of the rap song on Public Enemy's second album, *It Takes a Nation of Millions to Hold Us Back* (1988).

2. On the complexity of dancehall music, see for example, D. Noble, 2000, "Ragga Music: Dis/Respecting Black Women and Dis/Reputable Sexualities," in *Unsettled Multiculturalisms: Diasporas, Entanglements, Transruptions*, ed. Barnor Hesse, 148–169 (New York: Zed Books); Carolyn Cooper, 1995, *Noises in the Blood: Orality, Gender, and the "Vulgar Body" of Jamaican Popular Culture* (Durham, N.C.: Duke University Press); and D. P. Hope, 2006, *Inna di Dancehall: Popular Culture and the Politics of Identity in Jamaica* (Kingston, Jamaica: University of the West Indies Press). With respect to hip-hop culture, see, for example, Ruth Nicole Brown and Chamara Jewel Kwakye, 2012, *Wish to Live: The Hip-Hop Feminism Pedagogy Reader* (New York: Peter Lang Publishing); Gwendolyn Pough, 2004, *Check It While I Wreck It: Black Womanhood, Hip-Hop Culture, and the Public Sphere* (Boston: Northeastern University Press); and Joan Morgan, 2000, *When Chicken-Heads Come Home to Roost: A Hip-Hop Feminist Breaks it Down* (New York: Simon & Schuster).

3. For example, passports are now needed to travel internationally.

4. Familiarity with the "Ghetto Story" video will help readers follow this discussion. It can be viewed online at YouTube at http://www.youtube.com/watch?v=loPRsrqrDXc (accessed 15 November 2013). Lyrics are transcribed at www.sing365.com/music/lyric.nsf/Ghetto-Story-Chapter-2-ft-Cham-lyrics-Alicia-Keys/AA350CB75F33DBB7482571D9000826FD (accessed 15 November 2013). Thank you to Donovan (Chris) Flynn for bringing my attention to the song.

5. "Ghetto Story," words and music by Dave Kelly and Dameon Beckett © 2006 EMI Music Publishing LTD. All Rights for the U.S. and Canada Controlled and Administered by EMI Blackwood Music Inc. Reprinted by permission of Hal Leonard Corporation.

6. Ibid.

7. Ibid.

8. Ibid.

9. Ibid.

REFERENCES

Baby Cham featuring Alicia Keys. 2006. "Ghetto Story" (music video). Atlantic Records.

Black, Stephanie, dir. 2001. *Life and Debt*. Tuff Gong Pictures Production.

Flynn, K. 2011. *Moving beyond Borders: Black Canadian and Caribbean Women in the Diaspora*. Toronto: University of Toronto Press.

Flynn, K. 2008. "'I'm Glad that Someone Is Telling the Nursing Story': Writing Black Women's History." *Journal of Black Studies* 38(3): 443–60.

Flynn, K. 2004. "Experience and Identity: Black Immigrant Nurses to Canada, 1950–1980." In *Sisters or Strangers: Immigrant, Ethnic, and Racialized Women in Canadian History*, edited by Marlene Epp, Franca Iacovetta, and Frances Swyripa, 381–398. Toronto: University of Toronto Press.

Khalideen, R., and N. Khalideen. 2002. "Caribbean Women in Globalization and Economic Restructuring." *Canadian Woman Studies* 21(4): 108–15.

Mohanty, C. 1991. "Under Western Eyes: Feminist Scholarship and Colonial Discourses." In *Third World Women and the Politics of Feminism*, ed. Chandra Talpade Mohanty, Ann Russo, and Lourdes Torres, 51–80. Indianapolis: Indiana University Press.

EXPERIENCING HISTORIES OF THE CITY

Mark D. Steinberg
Department of History

In my teaching and research I am especially interested in small stories, in the fragments and scattered puzzle pieces the past leaves behind, asking myself and my students how to connect these fragments to larger pictures. It is fine to start with large interpretive questions: in the study of Russian history these might be questions about how the autocracy and empire survived so long, what caused the revolutions of 1917 and brought the Bolsheviks to power, or how to explain the Stalinist Terror. I have found it more fruitful to work toward the answers to such questions through smaller stories—which, after all, is how most people experience history.

As a historian, I want students to experience the diversity of other lives by studying times and places different from their own. What has surprised me, but I have come to value, is how students insist on seeing connections to their own lives, to our own times, and how this helps them see the past in fresh ways. I want students to experience the same excitement of discovery and analysis that I find in my own research: seeing connections and patterns in the evidence left of the past and continually asking questions, including about our own questions and assumptions. What they see as they connect their own experiences to the past can surprise me, stimulating me to continually question how I approach the past as a researcher, including how my own experiences shape what I see and the stories I tell. While writing a book about the Russian imperial capital in the years before the 1917 revolution, I developed a new course, Exploring the Modern City (which focuses on London, Paris, Berlin, and St. Petersburg from roughly the 1840s through the 1930s). The book and the course took shape together, simultaneously. The story of their creation illustrates the way I approach the discipline of history.

For instance, I asked students to read a newspaper report I had recently encountered, hoping they would share my excitement in stumbling upon it and see the interpretive opportunities it offered. I found it one day while working my way through a yellowed and fragile bound copy of the popular daily newspaper, *Petersburgskii listok* (the Petersburg sheet), preserved in the newspaper hall of the former Imperial Public Library in St. Petersburg. The story was one of many "adventures" and "incidents" of city life that newspapers recorded, ranging from tram accidents to street fights. I was looking for stories ("evidence") that might answer my research questions or prompt new ones. One day in January 1910, I read, a merchant from out of town arrived by train at one of the main railroad stations of the capital city. Walking to a nearby hotel, he was approached by two "respectably dressed" young women, complete strangers. One woman warmly embraced the merchant, kissing him on both cheeks, welcoming him to town, while the other started going through his pockets. When he started to shout for help, the woman kissed him tightly on the mouth until her collaborator extricated his wallet and both then fled the scene. I copied the story on note cards, for I recognized it as part of a pattern of confidence games played out in the streets of the "city of strangers." Then I moved on to other stories.

As my students began to interpret this story as evidence, they enjoyed the cleverness of the criminals, including how they could transform their femininity into a type of power. They marveled that kisses and embraces can be weapons. They laughed at the naive small-town merchant, feeling their own superiority of knowledge about the wiles of the city, which Russian newspapers were also trying to encourage in their readers so they would not fall for the confidence games that were everywhere in play on city streets. In many ways this was a story about seeing. Just as the naive merchant from the provinces was fooled by stereotypes in his mind—respectable dress means a respectable person; women are not aggressive—part of the challenge of living in cities is learning to see beyond public masks and our own expectations. Some of the historical studies we discussed in class helped students understand this story. But they also found connections to their own experiences with crime news and with confidence games using email and the internet. Together, drawing on all our knowledge, we began to turn our interpretation of this story into an historical argument. In this case, an odd and amusing tale could be combined with similar ones to reveal the ubiquity of strangers, uncertainty, illusion, and the unknown that make modern cities like St. Petersburg both alluring and dangerous. Of course, I did not see all these meanings at first, and neither did my students. It was our continual research and discussion of sources and contexts that led us to fuller understanding. After considering this little story with my students over several semesters of teaching the new course, I completed the "Masks" chapter in my book. In it, the January 1910 story figures in an analysis of both local Russian and comparative ideas about modernity as defined by uncertainty, illegibility, illusion, and the unknown.

The history of cities is rich in stories like this, each an opportunity to think about bigger questions. Like me, students in my Modern Cities course were fascinated, for example, by the nineteenth-century Parisian flaneur—a man of leisure who would stroll city streets taking in every sight, feeling at home in the crowd, reveling in the city's special beauty, confident in his mastery of city knowledge. Few of the students had even heard the word before they entered my class. But before long, they talked about trying to act the flaneur when in Chicago or other cities during break. This approach is fun and different, but it is also a way to see and experience more. Of course, they responded to my questions about the social and cultural meanings of the flaneur. But mostly they were attracted to his style, to his way of moving slowly and attentively through the city. In a way, this is the purpose of teaching: to encourage students to take the time to look more acutely at things, to make connections, and to wonder.

When the city stories we examined involved sex or violence, as many do, the students were especially alert. I was uncomfortable with how fascinated students were with the most sensational stories from the past, such as those about Jack the Ripper. But these also allowed us to ask difficult questions. For example, we often encountered stories about prostitutes. Like people in the past, the students tended to view prostitutes as victims of harsh circumstances and the evil of others. But then they had to think about the many examples of prostitutes said to be "shameless," "saucy," and "bold," who refused to feel like victims, who evidently treated sex as a commercial transaction in which they held power. These stories led students to consider their own assumptions, and those of people in the past, and inspired discussions about the public sphere, economic life, the individual, and gender. Their observations were often remarkably thoughtful—and never purely about the past. Stories that made them uneasy, such as about suicide "epidemics," or pointless barroom stabbings between friends, or the prurient fascination that dead bodies in the morgue held for Parisian crowds, also inspired them to some of their best thinking. As we repeatedly encountered dark city stories like these, but also stories of fun and pleasure, they became increasingly ready for my typical question: what do we learn from such stories?

Newspapers play a major part in my recent research and in this class. For the final project, I asked students to write a "study of city life based on a close reading of one month of any big city newspaper." This assignment, which they thought initially sounded fun, gradually began to worry them. How does one find "history" in the space of a month of news reporting? Their concern increased when I told them that their focus must be not on national and international stories but on everyday "city stories." I even suggested that the best periods to examine (they begin by sampling different newspapers and different times) are when nothing big was happening at all, the better to capture history as it was experienced in the uneventful, uncoordinated, and immediate way we experience it most of the time.

Journalists have called newspapers "the first draft of history"—not raw facts or pure experience, but also not yet a well-crafted and orderly interpretation. Cultural historians have described newspapers as "cognitive maps," as analogous to the "flâneur's roving eye," as voyeurism for the masses (allowing every reader to peer into dark corners and private lives), as a fabricated "reality" that favors the sensational and cares little for the proper boundary between objective facts and plausible fictions. In researching my book, I found newspapers to be both rich sources of past experience and evidence for how isolated facts were put together, already in the past, into connected and meaningful stories. In class, we talked a lot about what sort of "knowledge" newspapers create, how *they* see and shape the ways *we* see the past. I still face the same questions, in my scholarly writing and in preparing for class discussions, when searching for significant stories and evidence in the pages of old newspapers or in letters, petitions, police reports, and other documents preserved in archives: how to turn the disorderly, partial, and uncertain fragments of the past into history.

Herman Hesse wrote that studying history means "submitting to chaos" while believing there is "order and meaning." When starting their newspaper research, students in my cities course mostly saw the chaos. I insisted that they read secondary sources about the time and place they had chosen, but these scholarly studies often seemed interested in matters other than what students find in the newspapers. A few bold students made chaos their argument: there is no order or meaning in everyday urban life beyond flux and incoherence (here they find support in some of the theorists of the city we read in the course), and there is even uncertainty about what is real. One student told the class—they briefly present their research, often with pictures, in the last weeks—that she could offer only the "intoxication" of wandering through this evidence like a flaneur, of getting lost in particular stories without offering arguments about larger meanings, for there were none.

But most students, like most historians, don't want to "submit to chaos." They want their research to say something important about the time and place they are studying, to have a recognizable argument, to discover order and meaning. Reading papers from cities like Chicago or Kraków, Bogotá or Mumbai (for they can write about any city whose newspaper we have access to through our library and whose language they understand), students connect the small stories to larger questions about the past (and not only the past). Many are fascinated by old advertisements, and find in them messages about gender (idealized images of men and women), race, and consumerism. Crime is a theme in many of the resulting student papers, and they read the evidence as connected to ideas about safety and danger in the city, about time and space (e.g., the meaning of night and of certain streets and districts), or about social class (e.g., how murder among the rich was described differently from murder among the poor). Even when students resist my suggestion and focus on major historical events—the 1906 earthquake, the 1967 race riot in Detroit, "the Troubles" in Northern Ireland, for example—they find experiences they had not anticipated: looting as a complex moral question, African American rioters' views of U.S. consumerism, how people made life "normal" during times of constant violence. There is something exhilarating, and profound, as students make connections, sometimes unexpected, between little stories and big questions, even philosophical ones.

I used to discourage students from talking about their own lives and today's world when interpreting such stories. I wanted them to try to understand how people in other times and places thought and lived. I wanted them to share the pleasure and work of historical research: submerging themselves in the chaos and emerging with coherent stories about what we can know and how things fit together. I still want this, and students value these goals. But they are never satisfied with mere "historicism," with viewing the past only on its own terms. They surprise me with the connections they make to the present—such as judging the gawking crowds in the Paris morgue in the 1890s as comparable to our own fascination with reality television and YouTube, or interpreting the outrageous acts of Russian "hooligans" in early twentieth-century Russia by thinking about graffiti on subway cars in New York or Chicago. Sometimes they see comparisons to social and racial difference and inequality in our own lives, to conflicts about how our public spaces are controlled and how some people challenge that control, to concerns about the entertainments we choose. I have come to realize that they are doing history just as one should. Trying out new questions with every resource at hand, ranging from what others write to our own experiences. And then there is the flip side: why study history if not to think more deeply about the present?

More than Creativity
Infusing Research in the Design Studio

William Sullivan

Departments of Landscape Architecture,
Natural Resources and Environmental Sciences,
and Human and Community Development

Design instruction typically emphasizes inspiration and creativity over other considerations. Although students are encouraged to meet the requirements of a client and often to do so safely and efficiently, the overriding emphasis is on novelty, imagination, and originality.

In a typical design studio—an enormous room with plans and sketches taped to the walls and the discarded drafts of those heaped on the desks, spilling onto the floor—students think "Creativity rules—I'm free to do whatever I want." As a product of this culture, I value creativity and innovation. But as a teacher, I want to inspire them to do more. From the first day of instruction, I bring research into the classroom. I ask students to build on our understanding from research to create places that enhance sustainability and human well-being.

An approach to teaching design studio that values a combination of research and creativity certainly isn't typical. It can sometimes rustle the feathers of people who see novelty as the priority. My approach is an outgrowth of an intense involvement in research for the past twenty-five years—I explore a variety of health benefits that having everyday contact with urban nature provides individuals, families, and communities. The health benefits are far-reaching. They include being better able to concentrate; being less impulsive, error prone, and irritable; having stronger ties to one's neighbors; recovering from stressful events faster; and even living longer than individuals who have less contact with nearby green spaces.

This focus on research also stems from my sense that it helps produce one of the most valuable outcomes of an undergraduate education: the capacity to think clearly and critically about ideas and the evidence that supports or refutes those ideas.

To engage students with research, I work to create an atmosphere of intellectual excitement—an atmosphere that provides a powerful motivating force for learning and a sense of hope that we have the capacity to overcome real challenges we face. In the following, I provide a short description of a typical design studio, identify two techniques I use to infuse research into the studio, and consider some consequences of doing so.

Studio

Recently, I taught the Sustainability and Health Studio course in the Department of Landscape Architecture. We met for three hours three afternoons each week, and students generally spent an additional dozen or more hours each week working on studio assignments outside of class. Learning in this course began with reading the empirical evidence demonstrating connections between specific landscape features, sustainability, and human health and then moved on to acting on this evidence to create designs for specific places.

During a typical day, we would begin by discussing readings—usually a journal article or a chapter or two from a book. We would consider who wrote the piece and what their motivations might have been for writing it, noting that the motivations of scholars writing about the impact of the built environment are often different from the motivations of the individuals who designed particular places and who now want us to understand how wonderful these places are.

Next, we would focus on the ideas and evidence presented in the reading. Which ideas are new here? What kinds of evidence are presented in support of these ideas? How do they relate to what we've learned already? How were the data collected and analyzed? Does the evidence presented in the reading stand alone, or is it consistent with other findings we've read? To what extent are the findings generalizable to other settings, such as the site we are working on today?

Following this thirty-to-forty-minute discussion, we typically turned to creating designs for a particular site with a focus on meeting a detailed set of physical, economic, social, and aesthetic criteria. For example, one exercise for a 200-acre site called for including three hundred housing units, a primary school, a mix of small-scale retail spaces and office space, and a large community garden. The students were also asked to retain all rainwater on-site, promote walking and bicycling, and to preserve the green spaces on half the site.

Before the semester began, I had developed an appropriate set of instructional objectives and created a challenging, engaging design problem that grew from those objectives. Once class began, my role was to offer ideas and evidence that the students could use as they solved design problems, to work with students on an individual basis to address questions, and to challenge them to include the ideas we had been reading about and discussing in their solutions. I also encouraged them to move toward more and more sophisticated designs. My students appreciated the demand, and most of them rose to meet the challenge.

I want my students to be creative. But I want their creativity to be bounded by knowledge that is produced through research. Thus, for me, the challenge has been to create a climate in which evidence from research is used in the design studio. Two methods have proved particularly effective: I introduce ideas and theories that are reinforced by research, and in the studio I use a technique called the Latest Story.

Ideas and Theories

The first method I use to infuse research into the classroom is to present subjects as *ideas or theories* and to emphasize that these ideas or theories represent our best understanding at the moment. We speculate about the possibility that these ideas will evolve over time as we learn more. In an effort to stimulate discussion and debate, I avoid simplicity and instead intentionally include ideas that overlap or conflict with one another. This is easy to do, of course, because our understanding of how to design and create healthy, sustainable places is developing rapidly.

My Sustainability and Health Studio students consider theories about attention restoration, landscapes and stress, and physical activity with respect to the built environment. They learn, for instance, about the relationships between the design of places and our capacity to pay attention and process information.

We rely a great deal on our capacity to pay attention and process information—it is central to almost everything we care about accomplishing. But this capacity has limitations. Perhaps the most important of which is that it *fatigues* (Kaplan 1995). We have all felt this mental fatigue. It comes at the end of the semester, or at the end of a long day during which we have directed our attention to a task such as grant writing, editing, planning, or teaching.

The costs of attentional fatigue (also called mental fatigue) are profound and far-reaching; they include becoming inattentive, withdrawn, irritable, distractible, impulsive, and accident-prone. This is an uncomfortable state, but it is strikingly familiar to all of us who lead busy lives.

It turns out that physical settings have systematic and substantial impacts on how quickly our capacity to pay attention fatigues and recovers from fatigue. Settings that require us to block out distractions, that compete for our attention, or that lack opportunities for small, restful experiences are particularly exhausting. But settings that include green spaces—even just a small plot of grass and trees in an urban area—provide opportunities to rest, renew, and restore our capacity to pay attention and thus function effectively (Kaplan and Kaplan 1989, 1998; Kaplan 1995).

We also consider how settings affect people's physiological stress. In small doses, your body's stress response is an amazing cascade of physiological steps that can protect you. It can save your life by giving the extra strength for self-defense or spur you to slam on the brakes to avoid an accident. But chronic stress can also negatively impact your mood, productivity, relationships, quality of life, and longevity (Smith, Segal, and Segal 2011). People who experience chronic stress are more likely to become seriously ill and to die at an earlier age than individuals who experience less stress.

Exposure to green spaces often produces feelings of mild to moderate interest, pleasantness, and calmness and these feelings can help a person recover from stress. That is, through exposure to nonthreatening green spaces, an individual's psychological and physiological arousal is returned to more moderate levels, which fosters an overall sense of well-being (Hartig, Mang, and Evans 1991; Ulrich et al. 1991).

Another important idea we consider is how settings can help combat chronic disease. In the United States, physical inactivity is the second leading modifiable risk of chronic disease and is directly linked to high levels of obesity (Ogden, Kit, Carroll, and Flegal 2012). One promising approach to promoting physical activity is to embed physical activity in our daily lives by designing neighborhoods and cities that promote active travel.

In contrast to fossil fuel–powered transportation, active travel emphasizes walking and cycling as the main mode of transportation (Dalton et al. 2011). One characteristic of a community that is both sustainable and promotes human health is that it provides for active travel in a variety of ways (Boruff, Nathan, and Nijenstein 2012; Guell et al. 2012). In the design studio, we read empirical studies that test the extent to which various characteristics of the built environment promote active travel and work to include the most successful ideas in our design solutions.

Thus, the design studio becomes a laboratory in which students incorporate recent research in their creative explorations. I have witnessed many instances in which insights gained from reading recent research resulted in a problem-solving breakthrough. One student working on a community design, for instance, had been struggling with how to meet what he assumed were conflicting requirements to provide high-density housing and opportunities to experience nature at every doorstep. He was frustrated that, when he worked to meet the density requirement, he was not able to meet the green-space requirement or that, when he sensed there was adequate green space, he was woefully shy of the density requirement. After several hours of toil, he returned to the reading we had been doing in class, and the solution jumped off the pages of a chapter on sustainable neighborhood design (Welch, Benfield, and Raimi 2011). Simply by treating rainwater as part of his green infrastructure system, he could easily meet both the density and contact with nature requirements. The innovation was to combine multiple systems (e.g., storm water, streets, and sidewalks, landscape plantings); the inspiration for the innovation came from the research literature.

Whatever a studio project's primary goals might be, we aim to ensure that the places we design provide opportunities for individuals to restore their capacity to pay attention, recover from stressful experiences, and incorporate active travel in a variety of ways.

The Latest Story

A second method I use to infuse research into the design studio is to present and discuss the Latest Story. This method refers to a very recent research publication that engages one of the main ideas or theories we have been examined.

One fascinating study I've used as a Latest Story came from my former postdoctoral colleague, Rodney Matsuoka. In this study, Matsuoka evaluated 101 high school landscapes in southeast Michigan. He then compared student academic performance among those schools, using a variety of measures, while controlling for a host of things that we know are associated with academic accomplishment (e.g., size of school, age of school, socioeconomic status of the students). The results were compelling: the greener the view from a high school cafeteria, the better the students' academic performance. Even after all the control variables were factored into his analysis, the findings held true. Matsuoka suggests that two mechanisms were responsible for these findings: students who had greener views were likely less mentally fatigued, and thus better able to pay attention, and students who had greener views were likely recovering from stressful events faster, which put them in a better position to learn.

Another recent study I've used in the classroom examined the link between exposure to neighborhood green spaces and levels of the stress among unemployed people in poor neighborhoods in Dundee, United Kingdom (Thompson et al. 2012). The scientists measured stress by assessing the concentration of the hormone cortisol in participants' saliva. Their findings showed that the greener the neighborhood, the lower the levels of cortisol. That is, the greener the neighborhood, the lower the level of stress experienced by these unemployed individuals.

I bring six or eight Latest Stories to the design studio each semester because Latest Stories help create an atmosphere of intellectual excitement in the studio. The stories help students understand that creating healthy, sustainable places depends on their mastery of the foundational ideas in our discipline but also on the emerging ideas that are being generated at a rapid pace. The Latest Stories also help us create an educational climate in which knowledge claims are viewed as fallible and evolving, ideas are questioned and tested, and inquiry-based learning is given a high priority. The Latest Stories also give students the opportunity to put new knowledge to work as they craft their design solutions.

Benefits of Infusing Research

It has been my experience that infusing research into the design studio underpins the development of high-level design skills and flexibility in problem solving. I suspect that my students develop more sophisticated, more compelling design solutions when they are grappling with theories and the research that underpin them than when they are simply instructed to be creative or original.

Engaging past and ongoing research has other benefits, as well. Given the pace of change in the world today, it is critical that designers stay abreast of a range of topics—from our understanding of human nature to emerging understandings of the health and well-being of the world's various ecosystems. The complexities associated with designing cities, business districts, neighborhoods, and parks require practitioners to be versed in ideas that continue to evolve. By engaging theories and recent research related to healthy, sustainable places, I work to model two dispositions that I hope my students will carry with them in their own work. First, I model intellectual engagement in our discipline, including an approach of analytical skepticism in the evaluation of all research. Second, I model the value of lifelong learning and foster in my students the enjoyment of such learning as well as the awareness of how important it will be in their professional and personal lives.

Ultimately, of course, I hope that these practices create tangible benefits for society as University of Illinois alumni participate in creating healthier, more sustainable communities.

REFERENCES

Berman, M. G., J. Jonides, and S. Kaplan. 2008. "The Cognitive Benefits of Interacting with Nature." *Psychological Science* 19(12): 1207–12.

Boruff, B. J., A. Nathan, and S. Nijenstein. 2012. *International Journal of Health Geographics* 11:22, accessed 24 Nov. 2012. doi:10.1186/1476-072X-11-22.

Dalton, M. A., M. R. Longacre, K. M. Drake, L. Cibson, A. M. Adchi-Mejia, K. Swain, H. Xi, and P. M. Owens. 2011. "Built Environment Predictors of Active Travel to School among Rural Adolescents." *American Journal of Preventative Medicine* 40(3): 312–19.

Guell, C., J. Panter, N. R. Jones, et al. 2012. "Towards a Differentiated Understanding of Active Travel Behavior: Using Social Theory to Explore Everyday Commuting." *Social Science and Medicine* 75(1): 2333–39.

Hartig, T., M. M. Mang, and G. W. Evans. 1991. "Restorative Effects of Natural Environment Experiences." *Environment and Behavior* 23(1): 3–26.

Kaplan, R., and S. Kaplan. 1989. *The Experience of Nature: A Psychological Perspective*. New York: Cambridge University Press.

Kaplan, R., S. Kaplan, and R. L. Ryan. 1998. *With People in Mind: Design and Management of Everyday Nature*. Washington, D.C.: Island Press.

Kaplan, S. 1995. "The Restorative Benefits of Nature—Toward an Integrative Framework." *Journal of Environmental Psychology* 15(3): 169–82.

Smith, M., R. Segal, and J. Segal. 2011. "Understanding Stress: Symptoms, Signs, Causes, and Effects." Helpguide.org, Harvard Medical School, www.helpguide.org/mental/stress_signs.htm, accessed 4 Aug. 2012.

Ogden, C. I., B. K. Kit, M. D. Carroll, and K. M. Flegal. 2012. "Prevalence of Obesity in the United States, 2009–2010." NCHA data brief, no. 82, Hyattsville, Md.: National Center for Health Statistics.

Thompson, C. W., et al. 2012. "More Green Space Is Linked to Less Stress in Deprived Communities: Evidence from Salivary Cortisol Patterns." *Landscape and Urban Planning* 105: 221–29.

Ulrich, R. S., R. F. Simons, B. D. Losito, E. Fiorito, M. A. Miles, and M. Zelson. 1991. "Stress Recovery during Exposure to Natural and Urban Environments." *Journal of Environmental Psychology* 11(3): 201–30.

Welch, A., K. Benfield, and M. Raimi. 2011. *A Citizen's Guide to LEED for Neighborhood Development: How to Tell If Development Is Smart and Green*. Washington, D.C.: Natural Resources Defense Council.

The Maps on Our Backs

Thomas J. Bassett
Department of Geography
and Geographic Information Science

The slide on the lecture hall screen high above me shows Donisongui Silué, who I first met in 1981—a strong, well-built cotton farmer in northern Côte d'Ivoire. Hundreds of students stare at the image of him handpicking high-quality West African cotton, for which, I explain, he will receive a pittance in world markets.

For over thirty years, I have been following farmers in Donisongui's village in Côte d'Ivoire in order to understand their agricultural lives and livelihoods in relation to the world economy. Like most cotton grown in West Africa, Donisongui's crop will be spun and woven in South and East Asian textile mills and made into clothing in Asia's booming garment factories. As a researcher and geographer, I am interested in tracing the multistranded relationships that result in poverty for cotton growers in the global South and cheap T-shirts for my students in the North. In my teaching, I try to make these far-flung labor and production relationships tangible to my students. The challenge is to come up with teaching approaches that help students understand the lives of people like Donisongui. My strategy is to use the same value chain method that I employ in my field research so that students can experience, ideally in a personal way, the same sort of discovery process.

The value chain approach examines specific links in the production process of a commodity in order to determine where value is created and who captures it. For a T-shirt, we start in Donisongui's cotton field and note the origins and costs of seeds, fertilizers, and pesticides, and the labor and machinery needed for plowing, planting, weeding, and harvesting one hectare. We could investigate the upstream production and exchange relationships involved in the manufacturing of fertilizers and pesticides and seed supply. Whether we go there, however, depends on which links we consider most important in answering our research questions. I am interested in knowing why cotton growers of West Africa receive so little of the world market price for cotton. Thus, I am more interested in investigating the downstream links like transportation and ginning costs, and the prices paid by cotton ginning companies and international traders for Donisongui's crop. But students wear T-shirts and want to know why they are so cheap, so we need to add more links to the value chain, such as the costs of shipping, spinning, and weaving of cotton fiber in South and East Asia. Then there is the garment manufacturing link, in which the costs of cutting and sewing cloth into garments adds value and thus affects the price of T-shirts.

When I visited Donisongui and his oldest son, Tenena, in December 2011, they were both pleased with the cotton harvest (fig. 1). The yields were good and the price paid by local cotton ginning companies was the highest it had ever been—57¢ U.S. for a pound of cotton fiber. But world market prices had quadrupled that year to $2.20 U.S. per pound. Why were Donisongui and Tenena getting so little in comparison? Farmers elsewhere were doing better. U.S. cotton growers, for example, were getting twice that amount ($1.25 per pound) (Simpson and Katz 2011). Why were the buoyant world

FIGURE 1. Tom Bassett, Donisongui Silué, and Tenena Silué standing before a mound of harvested cotton, December 2011, Katiali, Côte d'Ivoire. Photograph by Carol Spindel.

market prices not lifting all boats? I often ask such questions in both my research and teaching.

I teach a large introductory lecture-discussion class (300–500 students), Global Development and Environment (previously offered as the Geography of Developing Countries). This three-hour class meets twice a week for an hour and then in smaller discussion sections for another hour. These sections of no more than thirty students are led by graduate-student teaching assistants in classrooms or campus computer labs—depending on the topic of discussion. My biggest challenge is how to make students feel connected to relatively abstract processes such as the effects of world market prices on the lives of ordinary people like Donisongui and Tenena. One of my more successful attempts is to link students to the cotton value chain by having them do research on the origins of their own clothing. I call this exercise the Maps on our Backs. We read Petra Rivoli's *Travels of a T-Shirt in the Global Economy*, which takes readers from cotton fields in West Texas to lobbying firms in Washington, D.C., and then to garment factories in China and second-hand clothing stalls in Tanzania. Students are asked to select ten clothing items at random from their wardrobes and to record their list in an Excel spreadsheet. They note the item type (e.g., T-shirt), place of production (e.g., India), and the apparel company (e.g., Calvin Klein). For each class, the total number of clothing items runs into the thousands.

After teaching assistants aggregate their students' spreadsheets, they hold their discussion section in a campus computer lab, where students learn how to make maps showing the origins of the class's clothing. For most students, this is their first exposure to mapmaking and to the power of maps. They learn not only how to use the mapmaker-friendly software (Golden Software's MapViewer) but also about the many decisions that confront mapmakers. The principal question to resolve is how to classify and display the data on the map. This includes determining the number and ranges of breaks in the dataset that will signify which countries are the most (and least) important suppliers of student clothing. These breaks and ranges will appear in the map legend so the map reader can interpret the meaning of the map's different colors. I also urge students to select a color range that enhances the message they wish to convey in their maps. For example, a darker color suggests that more of something (e.g., clothes) is associated with that country. In the process of answering these questions, student mapmakers realize that they possess considerable power in shaping their map's content and meaning.

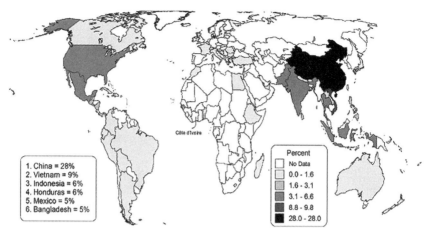

1. China = 28%
2. Vietnam = 9%
3. Indonesia = 6%
4. Honduras = 6%
5. Mexico = 5%
6. Bangladesh = 5%

Percent
No Data
0.0 - 1.6
1.6 - 3.1
3.1 - 6.6
8.8 - 9.8
28.0 - 28.0

FIGURE 2. An equal area projection (Eckert IV) showing the geography of clothing worn by geography students, spring 2012 (N = 2,143).

The results of this mapmaking exercise for 2012, based on 2,143 clothing items, appear in figure 2. As the legend indicates, the darker a country's color, the higher the percentage of student clothing produced in that country. The maps show that East and South Asian factory workers made two-thirds of the clothes in my students' wardrobes. Clothes "Made in the USA" were just 5.7 percent of the total. Once students have constructed their maps, they write a one-page essay describing and explaining the geography of apparel manufacturing displayed in their maps.

The 2012 map shows the results of just one semester's survey. What would a multiyear comparison reveal? Has the geography of apparel manufacturing (or at least the piece of it that college students wear) changed over time? Were more student clothes previously made in the United States or in Mexico? If there has been a change, then how can we explain it? To answer these questions, we need a longitudinal dataset. Thanks to student-generated clothing data and maps from previous semesters, that is exactly what I have. In a lecture I compare the maps from different years and ask students to look for any trends in the origins of student clothing. Comparing the 2004 and 2012 surveys (figs. 3 and 4) is illuminating. It indicates that some significant shifts have taken place in the geography of apparel manufacturing. What are these and how can we explain them? And why do these maps look so odd?

Figures 3 and 4 are cartograms, a type of map in which the size of a country is proportional to the variable being mapped. In this case, the size of each country is determined by the number of clothing items made in that

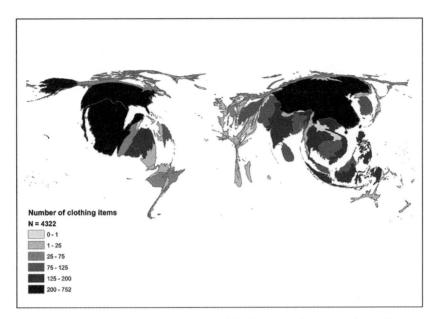

FIGURE 3. A cartogram map of the sources of clothing worn by geography students, fall 2004 (N = 4,322). The size of the country changes in relation to the number of clothing items originating in that country.

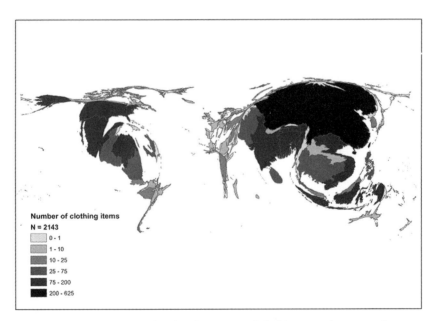

FIGURE 4. A cartogram map showing the sources of clothing worn by geography students, spring 2012 (N = 2,143).

country in relation to the total number of clothing items randomly selected by students from their wardrobes. I use cartograms in my own work because they are so eye-catching. Just by looking at the relative sizes of countries, the map reader knows immediately that more or less of something is located or happening there.

Figure 3 maps the results of the 2004 student clothing survey for which we had 4,322 clothing items. The bulging countries of Mexico, the United States, and China respectively produced 12.6 percent, 9.6 percent, and 13.6 percent of student clothing that year. Sub-Saharan Africa, on the other hand, is exceedingly thin. A comparison of the 2004 and 2012 maps indicates a regional shift from North and Central America to East, South, and Southeast Asia. In the 2012 map, the North American bulge has diminished; it now appears in eastern and southern Asia. When we look at the top ten sources of student clothing for these two years (table 1), two countries fall from the list (El Salvador and the Philippines) and two new ones are added (Bangladesh and Pakistan). The regional shift in garment manufacturing illustrated in students' maps has also been reported in the secondary literature (Dicken 2011). As a teacher, what pleases me most is to see how easily students make the connection between their wardrobes and the geography of apparel manufacturing. The abstract notion of economic globalization becomes more comprehensible and meaningful when students can relate to it in such a personal way.

The value chain approach helps students to visualize geographies of production and consumption that are often hidden when we buy things in our communities or online. Recognizing these relationships is the first step; the next is to determine how value and prices are formed at each link and who profits. As I stand between the students in their seats and the screen showing Donisongui in his cotton field, I struggle to convey in the simplest terms how markets work and for whom. One effective hook is the controversy over how U.S. government agricultural subsidies to U.S. farmers suppress world cotton prices (Bassett 2008).

Cotton growers from West Texas to Mississippi receive billions of dollars in price supports and subsidies each year. A perverse effect of these programs is that they encourage farmers to grow cotton no matter what the market price. Since U.S. cotton exports account for 40 percent of world trade, this strong incentive to produce cotton tends to drive down world market prices. At least this is what Oxfam argued in an influential policy paper published in 2003, which called for an end to U.S. farm subsidies to make trade more fair (Oxfam 2003). My students who hail from Illinois farm families feel uncomfortable with the idea of eliminating agricultural subsidies for the

TABLE 1. The top ten sources of clothing worn by students in the introductory geography course, 2004 and 2012.

Rank	Country	2004 Number of Items	Percent of Total	Country	2012 Number of Items	Percent
1	China	590	13.7	China	601	28.0
2	Mexico	546	12.6	Vietnam	188	8.8
3	United States	416	9.6	Indonesia	120	5.6
4	Honduras	195	4.5	United States	117	5.5
5	Indonesia	179	4.1	Honduras	114	5.3
6	Vietnam	173	4.0	Mexico	104	4.9
7	El Salvador	152	3.5	Bangladesh	97	4.5
8	India	139	3.2	India	93	4.3
9	Thailand	138	3.2	Thailand	70	3.3
10	Philippines	137	3.2	Pakistan	66	3.1

benefit of West African farmers. They argue that government support helps to preserve the small family farm, despite the fact that just a small number of large-scale farmers reap most of the benefits (Environmental Working Group 2013). We go back and forth on this issue, on what is fair and not fair trade. The value chain approach facilitates these sorts of local-global discussions.

Teaching students how to make maps unexpectedly turned *me* into a mapmaker. When I first introduced the Maps on Our Backs exercise, I was just learning how to make maps myself, since we no longer had a staff cartographer. Luckily, Golden Software had just come out with its user-friendly MapViewer, so I decided to make my own maps. My students' journey into mapmaking thus became my own journey. Within a few semesters, I became sufficiently competent that I introduced mapmaking into my other courses. In the Geography of Development and Underdevelopment course, my students and I made a series of maps on the geography of world hunger. At the end of the semester, we self-published a spiral-bound book of our maps (Lynn 2003).

While doing research with my students on the geography of world hunger, I discovered that a book on this topic had not yet been written. Around this time, a rebellion had erupted in Côte d'Ivoire that prevented me from doing field research there. Rebels controlled Katiali and it was not safe to visit Donisongui. It seemed like a good time to put new mapmaking skills to good effect and to write that book. I asked an agricultural economist colleague and friend, Alex Winter-Nelson, to join me. After five years of research and writing, we published *The Atlas of World Hunger* (Bassett and Winter-Nelson 2010). I made the atlas's maps using MapViewer, the same software that my students use in our mapping labs. My classroom journey into mapmaking had drawn me into a new research direction.

The Maps on Our Backs exercise enables students to gain a personal understanding of the winners and losers of economic globalization. By using the same value chain approach I take in my research, students are able to discover their place in the global network of labor and production relationships. Student data collection and maps are our start. From there, together we learn about how *we are all* connected, through our everyday clothing purchases, to African cotton growers like Donisongui and Tenena, as well as to Asian textile factory workers, cotton ginning companies and traders, apparel companies, and U.S. cotton growers. Making sense of and meaningful connections to these disparate actors and places is my primary goal in the Global Development and Environment course. It is a skill that students can take with them when they leave the university to engage with the wider world.

REFERENCES

Bassett, T. 2008. "Untangling the Threads: Africa, the United States, and the Cotton Controversy." *Illinois International Review* 7 (spring). http://ilint.illinois.edu/iir/online/2008/07/bassett.html, accessed December 16, 2013.

Bassett, T., and A. Winter-Nelson. 2010. *The Atlas of World Hunger.* Chicago: University of Chicago Press.

Dicken, P. 2011. *Global Shift: Mapping the Contours of the World Economy.* 6th ed. New York: Guilford Press.

Environmental Working Group. 2013. "2013 Farm Subsidy Database." www.farm.ewg.org, accessed December 16, 2013.

Lynn, A. 2003. "Mapping World Hunger: Students Create Unique Atlas that Documents World Hunger." *LAS News* (October), http://www.las.illinois.edu/alumni/magazine/articles/2003/worldhunger/, accessed December 16, 2013.

Oxfam. 2003. "Cultivating Poverty: The Impact of US Cotton Subsidies on Africa." *Oxfam Briefing Paper* 30, http://www.oxfamamerica.org/publications/cultivating-poverty, accessed December 16, 2013.

Rivoli, P. 2009. *Travels of a T-Shirt in the Global Economy: An Economist Examines the Markets, Power, and Politics of World Trade.* Hoboken, N.J.: John Wiley and Sons.

Simpson, C., and A. Katz. 2011. "Booming Cotton No Boon to African Farmers Milked by Monopolies." *Bloomberg News*, July 18, 2011, http://www.bloomberg.com/news/2011-07-19/booming-cotton-no-boon-to-farmers-in-africa-milked-by-regional-monopolies.html, accessed December 16, 2013.

My Education as a
Medical School Teacher

Richard I. Tapping
Department of Microbiology and College of Medicine

"You do realize that you will be teaching medical students." These were the words of Dick Gumport, a professor of biochemistry and an associate dean in the College of Medicine. It had already been a long day and an eventful second visit for me at the University of Illinois during which a formal offer of salary, laboratory space, and start-up funds for establishing my own independent research program had been negotiated. Now I was sitting in Dick's office trying to ascertain what exactly he meant by his statement. I should have asked him outright, but instead all I could muster was a brief affirmation. As I left his office, I wondered what I was missing. Was there something inherently difficult about teaching medical students? As it turned out, my education as a medical school teacher would be more difficult than I could have imagined on that day, but also infinitely more rewarding.

A year and a half after my conversation with Dick Gumport, I was standing in an amphitheater-style lecture hall ready to deliver my first immunology lecture to 125 first-year medical students who had recently matriculated into the medical school at the University of Illinois, Urbana-Champaign. These students were both eager and anxious as it was their first week of medical school, and they had invested a great deal, both personal and financial, just to be there. Arguably, I was even more nervous, having invested countless hours assimilating and organizing the intricacies of this entire, complicated system, which I had researched and published on over the last thirteen years, into some thirty-six hours of lecture material. As I began to speak on that fateful day from the pit of this lecture hall, 125 pairs of attentive eyes were fixed on me, and 125 pairs of ears were hanging on every word I uttered. But by the end of the course I had received only mediocre teaching evaluations, certainly not up to the teaching standards I had set after having invested so many hours of preparation. Students praised my background knowledge and energetic delivery but expressed frustration at the fast pace and seemingly disconnected emphasis on molecular detail.

The failures of this first academic teaching year could be squarely attributed to my limited teaching experience and my approach to the subject matter. I had delivered lecture material in painful molecular detail, information that only masked the larger unifying principles of this elegant system. Fortunately, the guiding principles, or central concepts, underlying the workings of the immune system originate from insightful scientific hypotheses supported by historic groundbreaking research studies. As I surveyed the rich research history of my discipline through this prism, I was more readily able to identify and emphasize the central concepts while removing the more irrelevant molecular details in my lectures. When delivered this way, immunology made more sense to the students, who not only acquired a better understanding of the discipline but also were able to begin to predict how the system would respond to a specific infectious agent or inflammatory insult.

Another major shortcoming of those first lectures was my failure to appreciate the educational interests and needs of my audience. As a basic research scientist I had little direct exposure to the clinical side of my discipline, but it is this area that medical students are eager to learn and need to master in order to smoothly transition from the basic science into the clinical years of their medical education. Fortunately, as I surveyed the research literature, I found many examples of how clinical study directly informs basic science. Many of the central principles underlying immune system function have been gained through clinical studies of patients with congenital immunodeficiencies. These patients, usually infants, suffer from recurrent infections due to an underlying genetic defect in their immune systems. As a scientist, I appreciated that the nature of recurrent infection in every immunodeficiency reflects the loss of function of a specific immune component that has been identified through painstaking research. What better material for teaching the basic principles of the immune system while engaging medical students in clinically relevant information?

Interactions with the MD-PhD students who work in my research laboratory have been highly influential in transforming my teaching in the medical school. For me, these MD-PhD students epitomized the integration of research and clinical practice in medicine, and as they complete the first-year medical school curriculum concurrently with their PhD training, I had plenty of opportunity to gain perspective on their medical education experience. I came to realize that the students were overwhelmed by basic science information without exposure as to how this knowledge might be clinically relevant and could ultimately make them better doctors. I witnessed their frustration firsthand and gained new insight into the necessity of preparing first-year medical students to see more clearly the connections between basic science and clinical applications.

As a medical educator, I learned that it is important to constantly assess the practical medical value of basic science course material and to make the effort to organize this material so that it is framed within a clinical context. For example, early in the first-year course, I used to present students with the intracellular signaling pathways leading to the activation of T lymphocytes, a specialized immune cell at the center of almost all chronic inflammatory conditions. During this lecture, the eyes of the students would glaze over with overt inattentiveness. However, since these same intracellular pathways are the targets of a myriad of immunosuppressive drugs used to treat chronic inflammation, in order to keep the student's attention, I learned to introduce the pathways in the context of the drugs themselves, their overall effects on immunologic activity, and their associated clinical application.

Basic research and clinical research are a continuum along which the former provides an experimental tool, method, or simply an idea that has potential application in the clinic. The clinical application of basic research findings can take years or even decades to develop, often ending in a series of clinical trials. Hundreds of research studies are published daily in the area of immunology alone, making it challenging to choose those that might be relayed to medical students. However, my training as a research scientist has been enormously useful in making relevant selections. For example, I introduced medical students to the vaccine against the human papilloma virus even before it completed final clinical trial testing, doing so not only because of its significant and unique clinical potential but also because the subject matter provided a single clinically relevant subject for introducing the topics of oncolytic viruses, vaccine design and targeted cancer immunotherapy. This vaccine (brand name Gardasil) is now licensed by the FDA and is successfully administered by primary physicians in the United States and other countries for the prevention of cervical cancer.

While it is certainly important to provide medical students with up-to-date information, this is a somewhat futile endeavor given the rapid pace of medical advances. This is especially true for first-year students, who are at least four years from internships and residencies and at least six to seven years from independent medical practice. In essence, it is instead more important to train medical students in the critical interpretation skills needed to assess recent clinical research studies. My firsthand experience in the research process enabled me to introduce them to these skills. After all, although different in approach, clinical and basic research are conducted through fundamentally identical processes in which experiments are designed and executed and results are critically analyzed with the goal of answering a question. These scientific analytical skills enable these future doctors to make better decisions for their patients based on clinical data from the most recent published research studies.

Learning about the first-year medical school curriculum through the eyes of my MD-PhD students enabled me not only to identify relevant course material, but also to recognize modes of teaching that worked for them, and to contribute to the education of medical students more broadly, beyond my own classroom and laboratory. Armed with this knowledge, I began to embrace a series of clinical case collections called Patient-Oriented Problem Solving (POPS) exercises. Each of these exercises, developed by the Medical University of South Carolina, describes a clinical case so as to enable a small group of students to work logically through the diagnosis of an immune-based disease (Virella, 2008). Talking to smaller groups of students in this setting and gently leading them through the logistics of the case was immediately more comfortable for me, but why? This had been my experience in the countless lab meetings I attended during my doctoral and postdoctoral training where research results would be closely examined and insights and critical feedback would be shared. As a primary investigator, I was now leading lab meetings for my own independent research group, and what I began to appreciate was that the research and clinical problem solving processes were quite similar. Both were driven by a hypothesis, either a research idea or a presumed patient diagnosis, which was tested through either experimentation or clinical tests. In a satisfying way, I realized that my basic research experience had direct application to the clinic as well as my approach to medical teaching. In time, my teaching colleagues and I would write our own POPS exercise on tuberculosis, which is now widely available to other medical schools.

The education of medical students through open discussion and cognitive tasks, such as small group exercises, is now heavily favored by the Liaison Committee on Medical Education (LCME), the national accreditation body for medical schools in the United States and Canada. These cognitive modalities, known as active learning, are now expected to constitute a major proportion of the curriculum while reducing the emphasis on didactic lecturing. Another active learning modality is team-based learning (TBL, Michaelson et al. 2004), and such exercises have been developed and are now incorporated into my first-year immunology course. During a TBL, the class is divided into small groups of students who work together on various course content questions or application-based problems. After this interaction, each group shares with the whole class the answer they chose, along with the basis for their decision. TBLs encourage students to formulate, convey, and share ideas in their own words, an act that promotes critical thinking skills and long-term retention of the information. Thus, the best TBL exercises are those without a single correct answer but with plenty of room for debate. Again, this is a familiar activity among research scientists, who actively debate various scientific theories among their peers at open sessions conducted at national or international conferences. A chairperson of each open session facilitates questions and discussion, a task that, in all practical terms, is identical to that of a course instructor facilitating a TBL exercise.

While my research training provided experience that I could apply to the education of medical students, I was completely unaware that the opposite process was also taking place. The most obvious manifestation of this reverse process has been the expansion of my basic science knowledge in immunology beyond areas directly related to my research. This knowledge has enabled me to more effectively understand and appreciate my research area within the larger context of the entire immune system. Moreover, it has enabled me to direct my research into areas of my discipline that I would have been unaware of otherwise.

My exposure to clinical immunology and clinical research, gained from educating in the medical school, has shifted my attention and research program into clinical areas with approaches more directly applicable to the human condition. For example, since joining the medical school, I have been increasingly insistent on conducting experiments with human subjects through the acquisition of primary human cells isolated from peripheral blood, bone marrow, or even surgically excised tonsillar tissue. My lab has also recently developed reagents that may find direct clinical use in the treatment of autoimmune disease. This clinical evolution in my research occurred at a time when the largest federal research agency, the National Institutes of Health, increased its funding for translational research projects with direct application to human health. My research grants did well in this environment not only because my research was more clinically focused, but also because I was comfortable writing and framing it within this context.

Sadly, Dick Gumport has passed away, but his statement, "you do realize that you will be teaching medical students," is as fresh to me today as it was on the day of my second visit to the University of Illinois more than a decade ago. If I were sitting in his office today, a decade wiser, my response would be simple: "Yes, teaching medical students is a wonderful opportunity to learn and gain new perspectives."

REFERENCES

Michaelson, Larry K., Arletta Bauman Knight, and L. Dee Fink, eds. 2004. *Team-Based Learning: A Transformative Use of Small Groups in College Teaching.* N.p.: Stylus Publishing.

Virella, G. 2008. "The Medical University of South Carolina Hosts the National POPS Website." JIAMSE 18(2) p. 48. See http://www.iamse.org/jiamse/volume18–2/18–2_complete.pdf, accessed December 17, 2013. This letter to the editor of JIAMSE (*Journal of the American Association of Medical Science Educators*) contains a general description and list of Patient-Oriented Problem Solving exercises.

DANCE AND THE
ALEXANDER TECHNIQUE
A Dynamic Research-Teaching Design

Rebecca Nettl-Fiol
Department of Dance

"We should write this." I remember the moment in 2005 when my coauthor, Luc Vanier, and I came up with the idea to write a book. Both of us are dance professors, Luc a ballet dancer and I a modern dancer. Much of our time is spent teaching dancers in the studio, not sitting at a desk, writing. And although I had already published a coedited book and an article here and there, I did not consider myself a writer. But our excitement about the work we were doing together, and the urge to share our ideas with others launched us on a pathway that transformed the way we think about research, clarified our approaches to teaching, and ultimately resulted in a book that shares with others our discoveries.

I am a professor of dance, and choreography has always been the focus of my research. Working with student dancers turns my research into a venture in teaching, as well. So my research and teaching practices are intimately linked. For example, in the rehearsal process, I work collaboratively with my student dancers to create a movement vocabulary specific to and expressive of the themes I am interested in investigating in the piece. Coaching the dancers to fulfill the movement intent is key in the choreographic process, and likewise in the training of dancers. In both my choreography and my technique classes, I aim to teach my students to perform with a full range of movement that is dynamic, expressive, and virtuosic; I am also particularly interested in cultivating efficiency, articulation, and elegance in their movement performance. Traditional dance training alone does not always adequately address the subtle and detailed information about movement that I feel is vital for today's dancer, and that I value in my own choreographic work. For me, a technique that has had a profound effect on my dancing, and has come to underlie my understanding of dance and movement, is the Alexander Technique.

Developed by actor and orator Frederick Matthias Alexander in the early twentieth century, the Alexander Technique teaches people (not just dancers, but people from all walks of life) to move with increased ease and coordination. The method involves becoming aware of habitual patterns of movement that interfere with optimal movement efficiency, and learning specific strategies for improving overall use and enhancing performance of activities, from the mundane to highly skilled. It is referred to as psychophysical reeducation because it elicits the rediscovery of your original poise (think about the simple and buoyant quality in the movements of small children), and your innate resilience and mobility (as seen in the elegant movements of a panther). For many, it has resulted in major improvements of health and relief from pain. In my case, I learned a whole new way of working that alleviated previous chronic knee problems, and I developed an understanding of the body as a dynamic system rather than an assemblage of parts.

After receiving my Alexander certification in 1990, I designed and began teaching the Alexander Technique for Dancers course at the University of

FIGURE 1. Rebecca Nettl-Fiol teaching an Alexander Technique to a student. Photograph by Natalie Fiol.

Illinois. In my dance technique classes, I was also continually researching ways of implementing Alexander ideas into the class, both through the movement that I invented, the class structure, and vocabulary I used, and the manner of giving corrections to students. It is not a simple matter to teach these principles to dancers. There are many discrepancies in the teaching methodologies between the quiet, one-on-one, hands-on teaching in an Alexander lesson and the dynamic, full-out physicality required in learning dance. Dancers want to sweat, to feel they have worked hard, and indeed, they need to challenge themselves physically in order to improve. How do we bring these ideas together? This incongruity is a significant issue, posing challenges to finding ways to negotiate the first person, or experiential, versus the third person, or objective vantage points in teaching dance.

The book project with Luc Vanier, *Dance and the Alexander Technique: Exploring the Missing Link*, grew out of ten years of collaborating on devising ways to teach dancers the principles of the Alexander Technique in a way that would make sense to them, and would be applicable to any dance style. Using theories developed from the Dart Procedures (a sequence of movements that retrace the path of developmental and evolutionary patterns) as a point

FIGURE 2. Using Alexander principles, Luc Vanier takes a student through a range of movements. Photograph by Natalie Fiol.

of departure, we were excited about the direct links we could make between developmental movement, Alexander principles, and dance technique. The Dart Procedures were developed by our Alexander teachers, Joan Murray and Alex Murray, in collaboration with Raymond A. Dart, a paleoanthropologist best known for discovering the *Australopithecus africanus*, considered to be the Missing Link between ape and man. Thus, our own "missing link" was established: the Dart Procedures, and developmental movement in general, gave us a lens for looking at Alexander principles and relating them to dance.

For example, we can look at a baby lying on his belly, and then looking up, eager to try to see something in front of him. This lengthening movement can be applied directly to a dancer doing an arch, or in ballet, a *cambré* back. The Alexander principle of leading with the head and eyes and allowing the body to follow is applicable here. In another example, we can look at a baby that rolls from her belly onto her back (supine to prone). The head and eyes lead the baby around in a way that lengthens the body to allow her to flip over. Once over on her back, the baby "resets," or releases the back into the floor. This sequence relates directly to the ballet *pirouette*. Turning the head to spiral provides the impetus toward finding the erect verticality required in ballet, giving the dancer the chance to be "lifted" without stiffening.

In order to continue researching these theories, I designed a course that explicitly applied Alexander to dance technique, offered as an elective for

FIGURE 3. Rebecca Nettl-Fiol shows students how a baby turns the head to spiral. Photograph by Natalie Fiol.

students particularly interested in this approach. The pressure was off to provide the traditional model of a technique class, freeing me to reenvision dance training. Here I was able to workshop my ideas more directly. Students were my fellow researchers, working with the movement sequences, and through trial and error, seeing if the principles I presented made sense physically. Students also offered feedback through questionnaires. This same semester I guest-taught at Luc's university, which afforded the opportunity for him to observe exercises and concepts in action from discoveries I had made. This provided a chance for lively discussion and sharing of ideas. How did a concept that he was teaching in ballet relate to what I was trying to do in modern dance? Does the same principle apply? We persisted in pushing ourselves to refine our understanding.

Our idea for the book was to simply write what we do: write how we teach, and how we incorporate the Alexander principles in each of our dance technique classes. There were no books on dance and Alexander. We had already developed methodologies and were applying them continually in our teaching and presenting at conferences. We wanted to delineate the principles, offer detailed movement descriptions of exercises that people could try, and illustrate these on a DVD. That seemed simple enough. We

FIGURES 4A AND 4B. These two photos show the relationship of the toddler's natural movement to the dancer's more refined movement. The engagement relationship of the head, neck, and back should be similar in both cases. Photograph by Natalie Fiol.

developed an outline of chapters, presented our idea to the University of Illinois Press, and were on our way.

Since Luc was teaching at another university, we no longer had opportunities to work together in the studio as we had when he was my graduate student. But that was where the energy happened, the sparks that generated new ideas and discoveries, so Luc and I sought out opportunities to present at conferences together. From that day in 2005 when we struck upon the idea for the book, until 2011 when the book was published, we presented our work together at about ten conferences, developing a chapter from each conference presentation. The conference proposal or abstract would form the beginning of a chapter. We would arrive early to conferences in order to finalize our presentation, and then present the material to a group, usually in a workshop setting where our research was revealed through movement experiences. Conference attendees might be dance educators, professional or student dancers, physical therapists or other medical practitioners, or Alexander technique teachers or others in the field of somatic/body-mind practices. Those days together became a hotbed of engagement in the material for us. Bringing our own experiences of working with our respective students, and the writing we had done in preparation for the conference, we would show each other new movement exercises, illustrate applications to dance movements, and share things that worked or things that didn't.

We also devised ways to teach together at our respective universities and were invited to give workshops at other dance departments, as well. One of the most fertile times was a two-week stay in Australia to present our work at the International Association of Dance Medicine and Science (IADMS) conference in Canberra, with a day at the Australian Ballet School in Melbourne. Here we had a chance to try our theories on diverse groups in an unfamiliar country. We were working on chapter 5, "Spirals for Connectivity and Lengthening." Our workshop was a hit! Doctors, physical therapists, Australian aboriginal dancers, and ballet teachers all seemed to be excited about our work. At a visit to the Australian Ballet School, we observed physical therapists working with injured ballet students. Seeing that we were in the room (and having had our IADMS workshop), they asked us to work with a young dancer who was having neck problems. Everyone gathered around as Luc began working with him, and in no time at all, improvements were evident to both the dancer and the observers. There was something magical overall about our time in Australia, the birthplace of F. M. Alexander. The experience boosted our confidence in what we were discovering and in our ability to design a coherent line of inquiry for teaching the principles we had been developing, and it invigorated our writing and propelled us onward!

In these ways, we continued our writing process. Skyping was an important part of our meeting routine, so that we could show each other what we were doing or demonstrate part of an exercise. At each step along the way, we hammered out and clarified the principles together. Much of this occurred around the movement explorations we were including in the book. In order to clearly write a movement sequence, we had to be excruciatingly specific about the intent of each movement. How does it initiate? What is the sequence? Does the focus lead the movement? Where is the emphasis? Is there timing involved? All of these elements became extremely important, and talking about them helped us understand more clearly both the movement sequences themselves and the underlying concepts.

In 2009 much of the writing was complete, and we were ready to shoot the video for the DVD. Working with limited funds, we hired five students to be the demonstrators and two student videographers for the five-day shoot. An important factor to us was to find a way to demonstrate the movement sequences with different types of bodies of diverse abilities, and with various amounts of experience with the Alexander Technique. In this way, we felt it would discourage people from trying to see the "right" way to do the movement or the "right" body. We wanted to show the movement itself, rather than the particular person doing the movement. So we used an informal, workshop approach for each section. We chose the lobby of the Great Hall in the Krannert Center for the Performing Arts, a beautiful space with natural light, white carpet, and marble staircase. At one point during our shoot, a toddler and her parents ventured into our space. They had just eaten lunch in the restaurant in the lobby, and the adorable little girl was playing with an orange. We immediately stopped everything we were doing and all cameras turned to her. Here we had our developmental movement examples clearly in front of us! As she joyfully twirled and twisted, we were able to see the connections we had been talking about between a roll on the floor and a pirouette in dance. She gave us beautiful demonstrations and taught our dance students a thing or two about natural movement. Although we had already planned to videotape babies, this magical and serendipitous moment resulted in some of our favorite images.

Toward the end of our writing process, Luc and I carved out a week to get together in order to review everything. Here again, we hashed things out, sometimes arguing over details, as we often did throughout our collaborative process. But in the arguing, or in pushing each other to explain or justify a statement, we would arrive at a new understanding. This would not have happened without the other's input—our process gave rise to a result that was greater than the sum of the two individuals who took part.

FIGURE 5. Little girl with
an orange. Photograph
by Natalie Fiol.

Dance and the Alexander Technique: Exploring the Missing Link was published in 2011. How satisfying to have a concrete product, something to hold in my hand, as opposed to my usual experience of choreographing dances that slip away into the air once they are seen. But there was also an unexpected outcome for both of us. Rather than just expounding our work, the act of writing the book had significantly and dramatically deepened our knowledge. It was in our conversations, in presenting our work at conferences, in team teaching, and in hashing out our ideas as we wrote them where realizations were made, theories established, and practices developed. Our conception of research also changed. Research doesn't have to mean locking yourself in a room and sitting at a computer, writing. Active engagement with our students and with each other created an energetic and dynamic process that not only generated innovative methodologies for teaching dance but also taught us to become daily researchers through our teaching.

Five Things Only I Care About

Carol Spindel
Department of English

Thanks to my students' essays, I understand how playing the villain in a video game can mitigate the boredom of a summer job in a warehouse (while stacking boxes, you dream up ways to take other players hostage) and the way to use a cell phone to avoid someone you encounter while walking to class (pretend your mother is calling). My students' writing has given me insights into what it's like when your father is laid off from his corporate job or your mother suffers from a chronic illness. And then there is courtship: how Facebook makes a long-distance flirtation seem like the real thing; how a severe allergy to peanuts complicates a first kiss; how easy it is to think you're in love with a hallmate who dishes up gourmet microwave cuisine at four A.M.

Students in my nonfiction writing classes have plenty of experiences to turn into personal essays, and their observations about coming of age in our society are often incisive and insightful. But before they can turn their lives into literature, they have to learn to pick out, from their multitudes of ideas, observations, and experiences, what they want to write about. How-to-write books often talk about finding one's voice, but far more important, it seems to me, is finding one's subject.

For twenty years I have taught writing classes at the University of Illinois in creative nonfiction and the personal essay. These classes are part workshop, part seminar, and part obstacle course. Gathered around a large table, we write together, listen to new work, and provide suggestions and encouragement like other creative writing workshops. As in other seminars, we read contemporary nonfiction to find models of good writing. The obstacle course is a series of writing exercises and revisions. I impose word limits, steer students toward concreteness and specificity, and nudge them away from the clichéd, the abstract, and the general. They write their way through these challenges to become stronger writers and to receive credit for the class.

The freedom to write about any subject can be exhilarating, but the possibilities can also be overwhelming. So we start from scratch. The first writing exercises we do together are intended to identify our passions, obsessions, and obscure little corners of expertise, to name and narrow our inquiries, to put a finger on what mystifies, fascinates, astonishes us. My students and I swing our flashlights wildly into the dark, hunting for things that gleam back at us. Our blunt instrument for this purpose is the List of Five. We aim for five entries on each list. Five Things Only I Care About. Five Questions I Keep Asking. Five Things about Our Society that Drive Me Crazy. Five Conversations that Changed My Mind. Five Moments that Made Me Realize Life Isn't Fair. Five Small Things I Am Expert At.

Although this sounds simple, it goes to the very heart of the writing life. You can start with the generic, *What is my subject?* but then you have to ask the more specific question, *Of my many various and possible subjects, which one is suitable, workable for a short essay?* At first, students often choose something like their evolving religious identity or a lifelong relationship with a best friend. These topics are doomed to fail. Their size makes them unwieldy. It's like trying to stuff a room-sized canvas tarp into a small duffle bag.

They are also too mundane. Everyone loves friendship. If my student writers want to convey something fresh about friendship or religious identity, they have to focus on one little paint-splattered section of that canvas tarp. If they can do justice to one corner, their writing about the fragment will illuminate the whole.

In her book, *The Writing Life*, Annie Dillard says, "People love pretty much the same things best. A writer looking for subjects inquires not after what he loves best, but after what he alone loves at all." Annie Dillard goes on: "Why do you never find anything written about that idiosyncratic thought you advert to, about your fascination with something no one else understands? Because it is up to you. There is something you find interesting, for a reason hard to explain. It is hard to explain because you have never read it on any page; there you begin. You were made and set here to give voice to this, your own astonishment."

Of course, we all know what we really pay close attention to, what truly intrigues us. But so often, there are other voices inside our heads saying, *That? That doesn't seem important. That is such an odd thing to admit you think about! Better not write about that!* Part of the writer's job is to ignore such voices.

One of the pleasures of teaching is writing alongside students. Although I am more experienced than they are, I feel like I enter new territory every time I begin a piece. So my Lists of Five are just as important to me as theirs are to them. The fragments I jot down in the classroom have sometimes evolved into essays and radio commentaries. But I never expected that a subject would leap off my students' lists and over the table onto mine. This happened in the 1990s, when I had been teaching for only a few years. As we wrote in our classroom, the campus that surrounded us was in the throes of an emotional and bitter debate about the identity of our sports teams, the Fighting Illini, and especially about a performance that took place at the midpoint of basketball and volleyball games and during half-time at football games. As the marching band played its interpretation of American Indian music, a student dressed as a Plains Indian chief came out and danced. The regalia he wore was beautifully crafted, the music rousing, and the performance dramatic. Students and alumni adored this moment, when every fan rose as one to be welcomed by the student who performed as Chief Illiniwek. But American Indian students and organizations objected to this appropriation of their culture.

I ignored the debate until Chief Illiniwek showed up on my students' lists. In his orange and blue feather headdress, he was a giant question mark, he was a troubling conversation, he was a sacred icon to be defended. The entire class decided to write about him. But when they shared their essays, the facts contradicted each other. Some said Chief Illiniwek was fictional, others said he was a historical figure. Some said the Illini were living in this area when the French arrived, others said the Illini had never existed. I was baffled. I had lived in Illinois for ten years but knew little about the state's history.

When I asked my colleagues, they didn't know, either. The chancellor announced that Chief Illiniwek was not a mascot but an honored symbol, as if that settled the matter.

I found myself, whenever I had a spare hour, descending into the university archives. The archives were located in a room off a tunnel that ran between our two libraries and going there felt like burrowing into a dark cave filled with forgotten treasure. Fortunately for me, this cave was not forbidding, for it was guarded by a pair of welcoming librarians. With their help it didn't take me long to lay my hands on enough facts to sort out my students' essays. But somehow, that wasn't enough. I knew that Chief Illiniwek had been created in 1926 by the marching band and had become an instant hit, but what I didn't know and what I still wanted to know was, *why?*

In university yearbooks from the 1920s, I found student poems that conveyed a melancholy sense of loss and survivors' guilt. The young authors wondered why they were on this carefree campus when so many of their comrades were buried on the European battlefields of World War I. Many of these young men had been Boy Scouts. I read old Boy Scout handbooks, which helped me understand the ways Scouts had been taught to identify with American Indians. A basic tenet of this era was that American Indians were diminishing in numbers and would soon vanish forever, and so Scouts learned that it was their patriotic duty to "save" American Indian culture by reenacting it. I began to draw lines from Chief Illiniwek to other points. A line went from the first student "chief" to a national Boy Scout leader who, although he was not Indian himself, taught the Scouts American Indian dances. Another went to John Phillips Sousa and the marching band tradition. Another to Buffalo Bill's touring Wild West show with its cast of Plains Indian actors. Another line went to the university deans and coaches, who, seeking to build character in the state's future leaders, seized upon the mythical Indian chief as a model and imbued him with the qualities they wanted to nurture in their young charges. Chief Illiniwek began to make sense to me, and so I wrote an essay. This essay sprang not from my life, as my other writing had, but from my classroom.

The essay was published in a literary journal, which could have been the end of the story. I could have moved on to another subject. But I kept thinking about the parts of the story I had left out in order to get it down to publishable length and about the connections I still didn't understand. The next time I made a list with my students of Questions I Keep Asking, there he was again in his feathers and paint, dancing insistently on the fifty-yard line of my brain. Chief Illiniwek. How could the same symbol be perceived as both an honor and an insult? Why had tribal dancing been so controversial that the U.S. government banned it on reservations? How had some history vanished, while other history was cherished? And when does borrowing, such an ordinary human activity, become inappropriate? The more I knew, the more questions I had.

A friend asked me why I didn't write a book.

Someone should write a book about this, I agreed. But not me. It should be someone who knew about American Indians. Someone who knew about sports. This wasn't my subject.

I was doing just what I advised my students not to, listening to the voices that said, *Better not write about that, for you may appear foolish!*

"Would you spend a month writing a book about it?" this friend wisely asked.

"Of course," I replied, falling right into her trap.

"Then write about it for a month, and at the end of a month, you'll know if you want to keep going and write a book or not."

So I researched and wrote for a month. On the last day of the month, I was just as obsessed with my inquiry as I had been when I started. The U.S. history I had learned had conveniently left out or misrepresented the history of White-Native relations. Our past, it turned out, was more intriguing, sobering, and astonishing than I had ever imagined. I thought of Annie Dillard's advice that I always passed on to my students, to write not about what you love most (which for me was neither the history of American Indians nor sports), but about what you are the only one to love at all. And I had to admit that, although no one else seemed interested, this strange conjunction of history, myth, symbolism, and conflict moved me deeply. Moreover, I felt my community needed to read this story as soon as possible so that the arguments in the residence halls and student newspaper could be based on facts rather than wild feelings. My account became a book manuscript titled "Dancing at Halftime." I revised the manuscript for the University of Illinois Press, and the press's editors and expert reviewers approved the revisions. Then, without warning, the press suddenly returned the manuscript to me. Their reversal about the manuscript, they wrote in a letter, had not been made for editorial or marketing reasons, but because the controversy on our campus had become so heated. This was another chorus of voices saying *no*, ones I couldn't ignore away. But I had committed myself, so I spent another year working to widen the book's scope for a national audience, and finally, *Dancing at Halftime: Sports and the Controversy Over American Indian Mascots* was published by New York University Press in 2000.

The writing led me to work with civil rights and American Indian organizations to raise awareness about stereotyping of American Indians in sports. In 2002, I was asked by the one Native commissioner on the United States Commission on Civil Rights to draft a resolution urging non-Native schools to retire their Indian-based mascots. When the commission passed the resolution, I felt an enormous sense of relief. The movement to retire these sports stereotypes had been recognized as a civil rights movement by our government's advisory body on civil rights. I also felt a sense of anticipation. The path my students' essays had set me on was turning. Now, I thought, we will circle back to where we started—my own classroom, my own campus. Now, educational and political leaders in Illinois would have to acknowledge and respond to the Native Americans and their allies who for over ten years had been asking for retirement of the performance and logo. But the atmosphere on our campus had become so polarized that this did not happen quickly or easily. Native people in our community continued to be harassed and threatened when they spoke out, although I could speak freely without facing retribution. In other classrooms where students were reading *Dancing at Halftime* and in residence halls, I shared not only history, but also what I had learned from Native people about how difficult it is to live surrounded by stereotypes of yourself. I reminded non-Native students about the mission of a public university. I assured them that, no matter what other students might tell them, Indian people in our community and our state, national Native organizations, and the Peoria Tribe of Oklahoma, many of whose members are descended from Illinois tribes, all strongly objected to Chief Illiniwek. I also tried to make clear what a high price—in resources, reputation, and community—our campus was paying for its refusal to change. But many students had chosen sides and refused to listen.

In response to the Commission on Civil Rights resolution, the NCAA, the body that regulates college sports, instituted an evaluation process. Each college or university with a team name, logo, or performance based on American Indians was required to respond to a series of questions about the way the names and images were administered and marketed. Specific questions asked how relevant tribes had been consulted and whether they benefited in any way from the sale of sports souvenirs. Some schools immediately retired their names and logos. Others, such as Florida State, reached out to namesake tribes and sought to regularize their relationships; eventually FSU created scholarships for Seminole students. After losing two appeals to the NCAA the University of Illinois at Urbana-Champaign retired Chief Illiniwek's performance in 2007. The NCAA allowed the university to keep the team name Fighting Illini, on the condition that "Illini" be redefined to make clear that it no longer referred to an Indian tribe, imaginary or otherwise. Campus leaders did not provide an explanation of why the change was ethically right and necessary to students and alumni, so many of them continue, a handful of years after the ruling, to wear Indian-themed clothing and express nostalgia for the era of imaginary Indians.

Now, at the beginning of each class, my students and I sit around a big table, making lists. Five Questions I Keep Asking. Five Things Only I Care About. I encourage them to grab hold of their passions and obsessions, no matter how quirky, and write about them. And as I teach, I am learning to do the same.

CREATIVE CODE
IN THE DESIGN CLASSROOM
Preparing Students for Contemporary Professional Practice

Bradley Tober
School of Art and Design

"But I thought majoring in [art or design] meant I was done learning math!" This is the inevitable, and somewhat amusing, response that I receive from at least one student nearly every time I introduce the basics of coding/programming in an art and design course. However, my students quickly learn that, in the new and rapidly evolving field of code-based design, a little knowledge of mathematical principles goes a long way toward ensuring their success as artists, designers, industry professionals, and even future mentors. Just as learning code is a new experience for these students, art and design pedagogy that comprehensively recognizes and incorporates code-based technologies is also relatively new. My experiences as a design practitioner, industry professional, researcher, educator, and mentor have played a crucial role in informing my pedagogical approaches in this emergent area—in particular by providing me with unique perspectives on how immersing students in code improves their preparation for entering and succeeding in professional practice. It has become increasingly clear that designers must distinguish themselves with unique skills to compete in a difficult job market. They need to excel in an interdisciplinary and multidisciplinary field where code literacy is key to successful collaboration. Proficiency in code also helps designers move beyond simply generating ideas—it allows them to play a significant role in the process of executing their ideas as well (Tober 2012). It is for these very reasons that I took the individual initiative to learn much of what I know about code on my own, as I was never formally taught much of what I now teach my students.

My research interest in pedagogy that leverages the intersections of design and code, however, extends beyond merely recognizing these practicalities.

Code typically has been thought of as just another tool that designers carry in their toolboxes—a way of and/or a medium for executing design work.[1] In actuality, comprehensively integrating code-based technologies into design curricula provides new opportunities for teaching design alongside critical thinking and problem solving skills. This integration seems natural, as many of the commonly identified principles of design, including emphasis/hierarchy, economy, and rhythm/repetition, could also be characterized as principles of code. Focusing on promoting engagement with the code-based tools used to create software, rather than simply on the use of software applications themselves, empowers students as they develop critical awareness of both the discipline and their personal/professional practices—a result, in part, of both revealing and attempting to resolve a number of tensions that sometimes exist within the code-centric aspects of both practice and pedagogy.

Besides shifting away from learning to use specific software applications, which frequently involves conditioning students to accomplish particular tasks while doing little or no thinking at all, teaching coding can also be a more effective use of resources than teaching the use of software. Commercial software is expensive to purchase and just as expensive to keep up to date, both in terms of money spent to purchase it and time spent on training. Becoming proficient with code-based tools that are open-source and/or freely available is relatively inexpensive and a more efficient use of time due to their lack of planned obsolescence.

This efficiency is particularly important in a course like Design Foundations I, which all incoming art and design freshmen at Illinois are required to take during their first semester. The current course structure allows an individual instructor eleven class sessions to achieve course objectives that include exposing students to standard software applications, traditional techniques, and introductory art and design theory. In response, I developed a project, called 200 Lines, out of a desire to integrate code-based technologies into this existing curriculum that was otherwise only beginning to recognize and incorporate emergent forms of practice. Accordingly, the project can be thought of as transitional—that is, it addresses the new and emergent by reframing the existing and established. Over the span of four class sessions, students are rudimentarily introduced to coding in Processing, which is described as "an open-source programming language and environment for people who want to create images, animations, and interactions" (Processing 2013). Students use lines of code to render two hundred (visual) lines in a two-dimensional representation of three-dimensional space, experimenting with formal design elements and principles along the way. In my experience thus far, students begin the course without any programming knowledge and end having had practical experience with executing a project through code, rather than through more typical software-based tools. This, however, only occurs once I reconcile the tensions between my teaching (and university-level art and design teaching, in general) and my students' expectations. As first semester freshmen, the students taking this class come from an extremely broad range of high school art backgrounds, and most, if not all, have no experience engaging in practice with any concern other than expressing their individual creativity. The 200 Lines project is one of the first for many of my students to require that they work both creatively and effectively within a framework of restrictions—a major tenet of design.

In many creative disciplines, research often takes the form of continuing and active practice. Accordingly, my practice represents another avenue through which code enters the classroom. Successful designers typically have foresight—they are able to both anticipate trends and engage with them once they arrive. This is particularly relevant to research and practice spanning the intersections of design and emerging technologies, as it implies that designers must embrace experimentation with and exploration of these rapidly and constantly evolving technologies to ensure the designer's continued relevance to both the discipline and society in general. If designers fail to capitalize on the possibilities of new forms of practice, it is inevitable that non-designers will do so by creating work that society otherwise recognizes and accepts as design. Ultimately, this could result in eliminating the designer from the creative process entirely (Tober 2011). My response to this realization involves framing experimental design-oriented explorations of emerging technologies as speculative design—a manifestation of pure research that seeks primarily to advance fundamental knowledge, explore new possibilities, expand disciplinary boundaries, and provide a foundation for further (and perhaps applied) investigations.

I engage my advanced students with a speculative approach to design though a project in which they are prompted to create an interactive experience that targets a large-scale display (like a projector) and avoids the use of traditional human interface devices (like keyboards and mice). A number of students end up exploring and incorporating the Microsoft Xbox Kinect sensor, which is a low-cost device able to determine its distance from objects within the view of its depth camera. The Kinect was first introduced in the fall of 2010 as a new type of video game controller that tracks body movement, but multiple code-centric online communities quickly seized on the opportunity to explore alternative uses and applications for this new technology. I was one of these early investigators, framing parts of my graduate thesis research around exploring the interactive design implications of democratizing the Kinect. My course is not unique in engaging students with the Kinect, but the fact that this technology has made its way into undergraduate curricula in the span of only a few years is both astonishing and exciting. The tension addressed here is that designers cannot only engage complacently with the known and the established—they must be willing to chart (and learn!) the unknown and position themselves at the forefront of the discipline. This is a type of approach to teaching technology that must continue in order for students to have any chance at relevance upon entering today's job market.

In another assignment, my students produce an interactive storybook (in the form of an iPad-based web app) by augmenting their already existing knowledge of web technologies with just a few additional lines of code. I find that students are far more engaged with this project in contrast to some other type of assignment that is technically similar, but contextualized in a less exciting way. This contextualization proves extremely valuable as students enter upper-level courses, where they develop a comprehensive portfolio they will use to enter into professional practice.

An aspect of professional practice that is often uncomfortable for students is the sharing and reuse of code written by others (with proper attribution, of course). This is actively encouraged within creative code communities, yet there exists tension in the classroom as many students are apprehensive about working in this way. It may be that this approach feels less than entirely authentic, and in the art and design disciplines—where creativity and originality are often revered above all else—this can be difficult for students to accept. My students grapple with this in another assignment—one that involves the design and development of an interactive computer game. This assignment actively encourages and expects them to responsibly use the ideas and work of others. This includes using building blocks of code both that I provide and that students appropriate from sources freely shared elsewhere. It is then up to the students to analyze these blocks, understand how they operate, and synthesize them to form their envisioned game. This is a surprisingly effective approach to teaching creative code, especially in that it helps to reinforce good coding practices through exposure to working models of code. Students typically end up learning more about programming by being encouraged to use others' code than they would have by learning enough code to program a game (that would have been decidedly less exciting, mainly due to constraints on time and resources) entirely from scratch.

Perhaps the most important thing I have learned from my teaching and research is that integrating the two helps me and my students maintain relevancy in an area that is evolving rapidly. The futures of my students hinge on their relevance to the profession, which hinges on my relevance to them as an instructor and mentor. By ensuring my relevance to my students, I also work toward maintaining relevancy in my research and creative practice. In this regard, it is difficult to delineate between where and when my research influences my teaching and vice versa—they both seem to nurture each other in a kind of academic symbiosis. For me, this means that, in many cases, research is teaching, teaching is practice, and practice is research.

NOTE

1. Computer-based practices, in general, are not unfamiliar to designers. Undergoing transformations now, however, are the approaches to both teaching and applying the use of code-based technologies, which include tools used for web development: Hyper Text Markup Language (HTML), Cascading Style Sheets (CSS), and JavaScript; languages used for mobile application development: Objective-C (Apple's iPhones and iPads) and Java (on Google's Android platform); and environments for what has become known as "creative" coding—the programmatic creation of images, animations, and interactive experiences: Processing (based on Java) and openFrameworks (based on C++).

REFERENCES

Processing. 2013. "Processing.org." http://www.processing.org, accessed May 8, 2013.

Tober, Brad. 2011. "New Tools of the Trade: An Exploration of Interactive Computational Graphic Design Processes." MDes thesis, York University, Toronto, Canada.

Tober, Brad. 2012. "Making the Case for Code: Integrating Code-Based Technologies into Undergraduate Design Curricula." Paper presented at the University and College Designers Association Design Education Summit, Blacksburg, Virginia, May 20–21.

Cybernavigating

Kate Williams
Graduate School of Library and Information Science

When she and I met, Chicagoan Alicia Henry was a mother raising her son in Englewood, where she had grown up. While earning her bachelor's degree in psychology from Chicago State University, she also worked as cybernavigator at the West Englewood branch of the Chicago Public Library. She helped people using the public-access computers, providing just-in-time help and small, scheduled classes. Figure 1 shows her with a patron who returned to share news of her high school graduation. Alicia is a patient person who laughs a lot, including when she said, "some days after my shift I be running out the back door hiding, patrons steady after me!" Alicia was also an important guide for me in my research on local communities in the digital age.

FIGURE 1. Cybernavigator Alicia Henry, right, with a patron in the library. Photo courtesy of Chicago Public Library.

When what you are studying is changing rapidly, teaching has to stick close to the latest research. My own research focuses on how people in their everyday lives and in community-based institutions are "cybernavigating" their way in the digital age. Entirely new ways of working and living are emerging. Everywhere people are striving to catch up with powerful institutions that have already made the leap. The only way for students to understand this new phenomenon is to leave campus and talk and work with people, much as I do in my research.

Before describing how we do this, I must say that the University of Illinois is an ideal place to do this work. For starters, a land-grant institution is about working with people in local communities to make sure they're on top of new technologies, whether that's farming methods or using Google and Wikipedia. "Learning and labor" is our university's motto. Our early library school education featured a half day learning in the classroom and a half day working in a library. This made sense in the 1800s, when libraries were changing dramatically from small, elite book collections to mass institutions for learning and leisure.

But there's more. Illinois is actually world-famous in my own field of community computing, also known as community informatics. Before I even came to work here, I had heard about PLATO—the time-sharing computer system invented here in 1961 that was free and open to interested members of the public. Using PLATO, the public created online courses, played games with each other, used early versions of chat and email, and more. They had so much fun with PLATO that when I convened a daylong symposium, 50 Years of Public Computing at Illinois, folks came out again—brought a forty-pound metal hard drive 2 feet in diameter for show and tell, told stories, and enjoyed themselves. In the 1980s, the Urbana Free Library became the first public library in the nation to allow users to connect remotely to a university catalog—you could find and reserve books by computer. By the 1990s, two library school faculty members had mobilized people across Urbana and Champaign to use Prairienet, an updated form of PLATO accessed via the internet, hosting websites and discussion lists, and extending the technology-savvy area to encompass not just "North of Green Street" (as we call the engineering campus), but all of Champaign and Urbana. These encouraging experiments were running parallel to people at the university inventing the touch screen, the browser, and other engineering feats of the University of Illinois. Our campus is uniquely community-informatics-savvy.

The particularities of the library school here are also felicitous for this work. Prairienet was for ten years a center of research, teaching, and service: recycling computers, offering low-cost dialup service, teaching basic computer classes, and fostering other networks such as SinnFree in Rock-ford, Illinois, which helped move that town into the digital age. Cybernavi-gating is only the latest focus for community informatics at the University of Illinois, and is melded more tightly with today's core library services.

So when it comes to the current wave of technological change in local communities around the world, how does teaching link to research exactly?

Cybernavigating is the central assignment in Community Informatics (CI), the required course for a CI certificate and an elective in the Masters in Library Science program offered at the University of Illinois. I help stu-dents make a connection with a library, and they then volunteer there for part of the semester, helping people on the computers. Some students do this here in Champaign-Urbana. Others, particularly those enrolled in our award-winning distance education program, do it in cities and towns all over the United States and Canada. And still others have done it in their native China, when I have taught summer school at Peking University. So far, all the public libraries that students have worked with are like Chicago's—people beat a path to the cybernavigators at their local libraries just to be able to function in today's digital society.

As the students work, they write field notes. After they finish, they use those field notes to write about their challenges, their breakthroughs, and their reflections on the experience. In China, students work in teams, which allows them to create a photographic record of their experiences helping people. Figure 2 shows student Li Ran helping a truck driver. He had heard that it was possible to put music on his phone so he could listen to it on the road. They worked out how to do it on the spot. His amazement and gratitude, the happiness she felt helping him, and the series of photos help all the students put a value on cybernavigating.

I first met the Chicago cybernavigator Alicia when she spoke at the annual eChicago conference that I convene. It looks at how local communities are adopting digital technologies. The question is how communities can sustain themselves in the information revolution, fraught as it is with economic dislocation and attendant issues. Since eChicago is a campus-community conference, it brings community workers, local officials, librarians, students, scholars, and ordinary people together to talk about how their local com-munities are using digital tools of all kinds. What are the obstacles, the breakthroughs, the best practices? Alicia and four other cybernavigators were the conference celebrities that year—youthful, positive, solving real problems in their own communities. And my current students are always in attendance at the conference, absorbing what is afoot in communities similar to those they will land in as professional librarians.

FIGURE 2. Cybernavigating in a Beijing public library, captured in a student report. A student helps a truck driver put his favorite music on his cell phone. Photos by Yu Jie, used with permission.

My research has included focus group discussions with library staff. Each of these was organized for people in like positions, starting with the cybernavigators, trading a small honoraria for their reflections. As it turned out, many of them had never met each other, certainly not to speak plainly about their work. Scattered across the city, they were partnered with branch library staff, but they were not of the library staff. They are temporary workers on indefinite assignment in a library system with highly structured and hierarchical personnel practices; the library hasn't yet integrated the cybernavigators into the hierarchy. So while they have strong partnerships in the branches, they are also isolated. Talking over the adventures of their day-to-day work was a pleasure and a comfort, helping them theorize, or rather, make sense of it. Midway through one focus group there was this moment:

> Cybernavigator: "This is therapy! You're paying us to have therapy."
> [Everyone laughing and talking at once.] (Williams 2012, 56)

Alicia Henry, her coworkers, their patrons, and my students all helped me rethink the digital divide. Where others see it as a gap between computer users and nonusers, I see human agency and transformation as people overcome this divide by working together. I call it an informatics moment, and it's even changing the library itself:

> After witnessing hundreds of informatics moments unfolding before them, the staff and patrons at one branch library began to talk: Will the library be

a temple to books? A friendly place to use computers? Will it be both? As their cybernavigator explained, "I think, actually, we get used more than the librarians. [. . .] Everything seems to be online. So it would only make sense that, you know, with books came the librarian, and with computers came the cybernavigator, you know?" (Williams 2012, 70)

Another story told at eChicago one year illustrates this jolting change. Not too long ago, library staff were trained in book-and-periodical librarianship. Then databases, the internet, and public-access computers hit the scene. Wikipedia and Google changed the game of searching and sharing information. As librarian Roberta Webb told us, one day she came to work and found people lined up around the block. She called around: it was the same all over the city. The Housing Authority had announced that low-income housing applications were online and could be printed at your library. But they hadn't told the libraries. What a scramble they had that day!

The stories I collected needed to be shared widely in a popular format for students and community workers. Working with doctoral student Damian Duffy and art professor John Jennings, we produced a comic book (fig. 3). The stories communicated the never-ending stream of people seeking computer help, their frustration, and then gratitude. The comic is used as a textbook at the University of Illinois and as a training manual in libraries nationwide (Duffy et al. 2011).

FIGURE 3. A frame from the comic book *Cybernavigator Stories* by Damian Duffy, John Jennings, and Kate Williams. Used with permission.

The success of the comic and our sense of library transformation led us to create a logo that we share freely through Creative Commons (fig. 4). It expresses the "computers not books" aspect of libraries, and the "get help here."

In addition to cybernavigating, another way my students are exposed to additional reports from the field is via our annual Digital Divide Lecture Series, where ten to twelve local leaders share their digital divide stories. A different student develops a bio for and introduces each speaker, which helps to bridge students into the professional world they will be joining. And they are generally rapt at hearing real-world experiences from someone a little ahead of them on a professional path, in a sector they may have never come in contact with. There are many surprises. Greg Bruner, Illini Football video coordinator, explained that every single person in the football organization spends two-thirds of their time watching game video from the Illini's database of video clips—for recruiting, for training, for planning. His digital divide isn't the high-schoolers joining the organization; it's the one remaining coach who insists on VHS tape. Don Owen, assistant superintendent for curriculum and instruction for Urbana School District 116, explained that in the early days as recently as 2008, before new fiber was installed, he had to ask the entire school system to not use the internet for an hour so that one class could do an interactive videoconference session with schools in Pennsylvania and Africa. Michael Dilley, Urbana's fire chief, explained how companies are marketing text-based communications for fire scenes, but

FIGURE 4. At left, the well-known U.S. public library symbol used on street signs nationwide; at right, a symbol that communicates the new cybernavigating role libraries are playing. Left image in public domain; right image by Duffy and Williams, Creative Commons licensed, freely available for noncommercial use, with attribution.

firefighters are holding on to their walkie-talkies. And representatives from Urbana Free Library described how they set policies to limit computer use, but change them as soon as new resources are available; when they were able to try unlimited computer time, everyone's mood at the computers lightened up.

In sum, both students as they get their feet wet and people already working in communities need to talk through their concrete experiences of the technological revolution that's underway. What's possible in an institution like Illinois—land-grant, long-distance-educating, organized around research, teaching, and service—is to orchestrate these discussions and bring them together so that everyone learns faster and moves forward together.

REFERENCES

Duffy, Damian, John Jennings, and Kate Williams. 2011. *Cybernavigator Stories.* Champaign: University of Illinois at Urbana-Champaign Graduate School of Library and Information Science. Also available at http://www.echicago.illinois .edu/stories.html, accessed December 9, 2013.

eChicago. Archive of seven years of campus-community conferences on digital transformation in Chicago's communities, 2007–2013. http://www.echicago.illinois .edu, accessed December 9, 2013.

50 Years of Public Computing at Illinois. 2010. Archive of a symposium held at the University of Illinois at Urbana-Champaign, April 15–26. http://50years.lis .illinois.edu, accessed December 9, 2013.

Williams, Kate. 2012. "Informatics Moments." *Library Quarterly* 82 (1): 47–73.

Humanities and Sciences at Work
Liberatory Education for Millennials

Kyle T. Mays
Department of History

What is research? What is teaching? What happens when these two actions are fused into one? These were the questions that *An Illinois Sampler: Teaching and Research on the Prairie* addresses in eighteen different ways. Conceptualized by Drs. Antoinette Burton and Mary-Ann Winkelmes, this edited volume seeks to highlight the relationship between teaching and research, and how it leads to more informed teachers, students, and societies. In short, the production of this volume proves that when research and teaching are integrated, what we do in the academy is valuable in several ways. Faculty members become better teachers and researchers, students benefit from the expertise and careful attention to learning, and the public benefits from partnerships that connect developing knowledge with real-world challenges. This volume has succeeded in its basic endeavor.

Yet much more occurred in the discussions that produced these chapters. Unexpected to many of us were the strong parallels that exist between those who work in the humanities (and here I use the term broadly to include the social sciences) and those who work in the applied and biological sciences. The monthly workshops served as a space where humanities and sciences became intimately linked as groups of authors shared and analyzed their ambitions for their own students' learning. These discussions led us to an unexpected insight: the humanities and sciences are not all together different, especially when students' success is the central focus.

The Humanities and Sciences— through Students—at Work

One of the key moments when science and humanities came together in our discussions was during the workshop held December 12, 2012, featuring essays composed by Bruce Fouke, professor of Geology, and Luisa Rosu, research associate for Illinois' Science, Technology, Engineering and Mathematics Initiative, at the University of Illinois. In the roles of respondents to these essays were Dede Ruggles, a professor of landscape architecture, Julie Gunn, associate professor of music, and Laurie R. Johnson, associate professor of Germanic languages and literature. The conversation that emerged was not necessarily about teaching and research, but about how the two in combination humanize the scientific method and help the student conducting fieldwork or laboratory experiments engage in critical self-reflection. Our humanist respondents engaged our scientist authors in a comparison of how all of them view their goals for students' development as self-aware learners. As I explain later, a little yellow notebook helped.

This workshop was especially energetic. There was laughter. It was lively. It was fun. It demonstrated how science and humanities can be seamlessly integrated. It was also challenging for the authors and respondents alike. After about twenty-three minutes of critique provided by Ruggles and Gunn, our focus shifted dramatically from the mechanics and specific content of Bruce Fouke's essay to a conversational moment in which he reflected on how science and students become one. He conducts research all over the world, and uniquely his classroom is neither a large lecture hall nor a seminar room nor or a lab where everyone wears goggles and lab coats; it is around the globe, in the outdoors. Not only do his students perform experiments, they also compose self-reflections (in yellow, waterproof notebooks) on aspects of their experience that may have little to do with science. Our humanist respondents pushed Fouke to describe more explicitly his goals for his students' learning and development as scientists and citizens of the world. He wants his students not only to perform their fieldwork, but also seek to learn more of themselves within these environmental contexts. These little waterproof yellow notebooks contained both the scientific work of students and their human experience. What is even better is that, because they are waterproof, even if they fell into the sea, the science notes and the human soul crafted on paper would not dissolve nor fade away.

This was a wonderful example of how humanities and sciences can go hand in hand. You can have all of your scientific equations and notes in the field book as well as your personal reflections and emotions; those personal reflections are not necessarily about the scientific experiments, but how the self is simultaneously being shaped by the science and everything that goes into conducting fieldwork. The beauty of this process suggests that within this one notebook you have human expression and scientific knowledge. They are engaged in a beautiful struggle, each informing the other, and both as parts of the humanistic scientific method as Fouke sees it. This was a powerful instance for it shows how faculty at the University of Illinois are not only concerned with their students doing good work, whether or not students learn the scientific method, but are also interested in how the self is developed during the learning process. Black feminist intellectual bell hooks once wrote "to teach in a manner that respects and cares for the souls of our students is essential if we are to provide the necessary conditions where learning can most deeply and intimately begin."[1] If we as educators can continue to keep students central to humanities and science education, we might tap into the deep, creative thinking that is required in today's world, and might even assist in the development of the whole person, for the future benefit of individuals and societies.

Toward Liberatory Education for Millennials

The education of today's millennial students should teach them how to solve problems, think creatively and critically, and better their "community," broadly understood. We don't need simply the humanities or solely the sciences; millennial students need a holistic, liberatory education—one that betters the human condition. Who are the millennials? This is the generation born post-1980, who are now entering adulthood. They are more ethnically and racially diverse (if not in attitude, certainly in demographics). Seventy-five percent have a social networking profile. Although these generational lines are often arbitrary, at least one aspect makes millennials unique: their ability to integrate technology into their social milieus.[2] More importantly, millennials face an uncertain future, economically, politically, and socially. This is why it is important for teacher-researchers at institutions such as the University of Illinois to think carefully about how they educate millennials.

The authors in *An Illinois Sampler* collectively deal with one of the most important issues facing millennials: practical education versus liberal education. In other words, this volume challenges the idea that science and humanities are so different that they can't operate, if not together, at least in parallel fashion. It is the link between teaching and research as a single educational experience that unites them.

Engaging students in this unified experience is important. It breeds imagination and self-reflection. Employers desire ingenuity from their employees. They don't want employees who have been narrowly defined by an academic major, with little capability of thinking critically and innovatively. According to a survey conducted by the Association of American Colleges and Universities for a partnership between university presidents and businesses and nonprofits, 75 percent of employers want emphasis in five key areas:

critical thinking, complex problem solving, written and oral communication, and applied knowledge in real-world settings. Most business owners and directors of nonprofits surveyed believed that both a broad range of skills and knowledge is valued over a specific major.[3] In short, they value a broad, holistic liberal arts education—not an education that produces robots with only a narrow ability to solve complex problems.

W. E. B. Du Bois believed we should gain from education "a loftier respect for the sovereign human soul that seeks to know itself and the world about it; it seeks a freedom for expansion and self-development."[4] The authors in *An Illinois Sampler* represent a broad range of academic disciplines, united by their desire to educate students in such a holistic manner. This book should remind us that, when students become central, the humanities and sciences are not all that different, research and teaching are one, and the beneficiaries are students, their teachers, and our society.

NOTES

1. bell hooks, *Teaching to Transgress: Education as the Practice of Freedom* (New York and London: Routledge, 1994), 13.

2. Pew Research Center, "Millennials: Confident. Connected. Open to Change," executive summary, February 24, 2010, http://www.pewsocialtrends.org/2010/02/24/millennials-confident-connected-open-to-change/, accessed April 16, 2013.

3. Association of American Colleges and Universities, "It Takes More than a Major: Employer Priorities for College Learning and Student Success," http://www.aacu.org/leap/presidentstrust/compact/2013SurveySummary.cfm, accessed April 16, 2013.

4. W. E. B. Du Bois, *The Souls of Black Folk* (Chicago: Dover Publications, 1994), 66.

ABOUT THE CONTRIBUTORS

Nancy Abelmann, an associate vice chancellor for research, is the Harry E. Preble Professor in the Departments of Anthropology, Asian American Studies, and East Asian Languages and Cultures. Abelmann is an anthropologist specializing on the Koreas and Asian America, with interests in class, education, family, migration, mental health, and gender. She writes here about the relationship between her classrooms and her own ethnographic studies of South Korean, South Korean educational migrants, and Korean America.

Flavia C. D. Andrade is an assistant professor of kinesiology and community health whose interdisciplinary research focuses on the social, behavioral, economic, and biological determinants of population health over the life course, with a focus on Latin American and Caribbean populations. She writes here about how statistics can be empowering and exciting by connecting it to students' daily experiences and various research and life interests.

Jayadev Athreya is an assistant professor in the Mathematics Department, whose research focuses on geometry, dynamical systems, and connections to number theory. His contribution to the *Sampler* discusses the process of growth that teachers go through as they move forward in a career, particularly in the context of being comfortable with experimenting with new forms and techniques of instruction.

Betty Jo Barrett is clinical assistant professor and works in the area of socio-technical systems in the Institute of Labor and Industrial Relations; she taught the Leading Sustainable Change Course for the iFoundry program in spring 2012.

Thomas J. Bassett is professor of geography and geographic information science and a director of LAS Global Studies. He specializes in the political ecology of agrarian change in the West Africa savanna with interests in cotton growing, food security, land tenure systems, and environmental change. He describes here how mapping the origins of their clothing connects students in a personal way to seemingly distant global social, economic, and political processes.

Hugh Bishop is a lecturer in second language acquisition and teacher education at UIUC as well as linguistics, and directs the Language Partners Program in the Education Justice Project. In 2013 he was named Volunteer of the Year by the Illinois Department of Corrections.

Antoinette Burton is professor of history and Bastian Professor of Global and Transnational Studies. A Guggenheim Fellow (2010–11) and the author of several historical monographs, she has also written *A Primer for Teaching World History: Ten Design Principles* (Duke, 2012) and edited *The Feedback Loop: Historians Talk about the Links Between Research and Teaching* (American Historical Association, 2013).

Lauren A. Denofrio-Corrales is the assistant director of the Honors Program in the College of Liberal Arts and Sciences and former instructor in the Department of Chemistry. Denofrio-Corrales is pursuing a doctorate in education, with specific emphasis on socialization and professional development of scientists and engineers. She and her coauthor, Yi Lu, write about the development of a chemistry course that links students' scientific interests to cutting-edge research opportunities and models the workings of a scientific research group.

Lizanne DeStefano is the director of the I-STEM Educational Initiative. She is the P-20 Council Coordinator, a Fox Family Professor, and professor of educational psychology in the College of Education. DeStefano's research interests include the evaluation and sustainability of innovative programs, multisite initiatives, and programs serving special populations such as students with disabilities or those at risk for academic failure. She coordinated the evaluation of the iFoundry curriculum.

Karen Flynn is an associate professor in the Department of Gender and Women's Studies and the Department of African-American Studies. Her research interests include migration, travel, women, work and family, health, feminist and critical antiracist theory, and postcolonial studies. For the *Sampler*, she demonstrates her use of several methods in the introductory course Black Women in the Diaspora. She focuses specifically on dancehall while making references to rap music, to explore connections among Black women's lives across various geographical locations. Her book, *Moving* *beyond Borders: Black Canadian and Caribbean Women in the African Canadian Diaspora* (University of Toronto Press, 2011), addresses the themes covered in her course.

Bruce W. Fouke is a professor in the Departments of Geology and Microbiology, and in the Biocomplexity Theme in the Institute for Genomic Biology. He also serves as director of the Roy J. Carver Biotechnology Center. Bruce specializes in integrated geological and biological studies. He also serves on science panels and steering committees at the National Science Foundation, NASA, and the Department of Energy. Bruce's chapter makes the case that there is no substitute for educational experiences in the field, which uniquely meld science and humanity to provide the type of holistic integration needed to approach the most vexing issues facing our society.

Rebecca Ginsburg, architectural historian and associate professor in the College of Education, founded, directs, and teaches in the Education Justice Project.

Julie Jordan Gunn is an associate professor in the School of Music. She is a pianist who is drawn to collaboration. This has led her into the fields of art song recitals, cabaret, opera, European languages, song arranging, conducting, and chamber music. Although she loves teaching young adults, she has become increasingly interested in building programs for younger students that connect musical teenagers to mentors in the arts. For the *Sampler* collection, she writes about how performance and collaboration are intertwined and her conviction that they are powerful teaching tools.

Geoffrey Herman is a visiting assistant professor with the iFoundry and the Department of Electrical and Computer Engineering. He is the lead for the Intrinsic Motivation Course Conversion project, revising and teaching core engineering courses.

Laurie Johnson is associate professor of German with affiliations in the Comparative and World Literature program and the Unit for Criticism and Interpretive Theory. Her specialties are German romanticism and idealism, with interests in the history of psychology and psychiatry and in psychoanalysis. She is the author of *Aesthetic Anxiety* (2010) and *The Art of Recollection in Jena Romanticism* (2002). Her contribution to the *Sampler* describes the ways in which her experiences teaching a large humanities lecture course have informed and changed her research. She makes the case for the continued life of the lecture, even as methods of teaching and knowledge production inevitably change.

Yi Lu is the Jay and Ann Schenck Professor of Chemistry and Howard Hughes Medical Institute Professor in the Departments of Chemistry, Biochemistry, Bioengineering, and Materials Science and Engineering. He is also a member of the Center for Biophysics and Computational Biology and the Beckman Institute for Advanced Science and Technology. His research interests lie at the interface between chemistry and biology and in entrepreneurship and innovation in undergraduate science education.

Kyle T. Mays is a doctoral candidate in the Department of History at the University of Illinois. He is working on his dissertation, "And We Shall Remain: Reclaiming Detroit as an Indigenous Space, 1837–1994," for which he was awarded a Newberry Consortium in American Indian Studies Graduate Fellowship. This cultural and social history examines how race and gender are formed through indigenous peoples and presences in Detroit. He is the author of "Transnational Progressivism: African Americans, Native Americans, and the Universal Races Congress of 1911" (*American Indian Quarterly* 37:3, 2013). He also serves as the managing editor for the new *Native American and Indigenous Studies Journal*, published by the University of Minnesota Press.

Rebecca Nettl-Fiol, professor of dance, is a teacher, choreographer, and author, specializing in the integration of Somatic Studies in the teaching of dance technique and performance. She is the coauthor of *Dance and the Alexander Technique: Exploring the Missing Link* and *The Body Eclectic: Evolving Practices in Dance Training*, both published by University of Illinois Press. Her contribution to the *Sampler* discusses the writing process for her most recent book, revealing the symbiotic relationship that was developed by the coauthors between teaching and research.

Audrey Petty is associate professor in the Department of English, has published numerous works of fiction, poetry, and nonfiction, and has taught for the Education Justice Project.

Anke Pinkert, associate professor in Germanic languages and literatures as well as in media and cinema studies, has taught for the Education Justice Project and led a series of meditation workshops.

Raymond Price is the William H. Severns Chair of Human Behavior in the College of Engineering and the iFoundry codirector. Prior to joining the faculty in 1998, he had a long career in industry, as a vice president of human resources at Allergan Inc. and a director of employee training and development at Boeing. His most recent publication is *Serial Innovators: How Individuals Create and Deliver Breakthrough Innovations in Mature Firms.*

Luisa-Maria Rosu is a research associate at I-STEM; she is participating in the evaluation of the iFoundry curriculum in the College of Engineering. A former mathematics teacher and instructor, elementary through college, Rosu's research interests evolved from the professional knowledge for mathematics teaching to the representations of teaching quality in higher education. Her *Sampler* essay illustrates how principles of engineering research apply to iFoundry curriculum design and implementation.

D. Fairchild Ruggles is a professor of art, architecture, and landscape history in the Department of Landscape Architecture. She chairs the Education Justice Project Advisory Board and has taught two classes through the program. With her coauthors, here she reflects on the unexpected challenges and rewards of teaching at a medium-high security state prison.

Carol Spindel, a lecturer in the Department of English, has taught nonfiction writing to Illinois undergraduates for over twenty years through the Campus Honors Program and Unit One/Allen Hall Living Learning Center. She has written books about living in a rural community in Côte d'Ivoire, West Africa, and the controversy over American Indian–themed sports mascots, as well as radio commentaries and essays on many other topics. She is currently collecting the life stories of Ivoirians she knew as children. In her *Sampler* essay, she talks about how, in the process of guiding her Illinois students toward their subjects, she found an unlikely one of her own.

Mark D. Steinberg, professor of history, researches, teaches, and writes about Russia and the city, modernity, revolution, religion, emotions, and the development of ideas and values. He is also coauthor of a widely used textbook, *A History of Russia,* and is writing a new history of the Russian Revolution, which also seeks to combine newest research with value for the classroom. For the *Sampler,* he explores his experience of bringing together his research, teaching, and writing about the urban experience—a story of connections and surprises.

William Sullivan is a professor in the Departments of Landscape Architecture, Natural Resources and Environmental Sciences, and Human and Community Development. He examines the health benefits of having everyday contact with green places and citizen participation in environmental design. Sullivan teaches on campus and at the Danville Correctional Center—a medium- and high-security State of Illinois prison—and is an active member of the university's Education Justice Project. For the *Sampler* collection, he considers the challenge of infusing research into the design studio and the rewards of doing so.

Richard I. Tapping is an associate professor in the Department of Microbiology and the associate dean for research in the College of Medicine. His laboratory studies mechanisms that underlie regulation of the host immune response and how loss of this regulation drives autoimmune disease. Over the last ten years, he has taught the discipline of immunology to medical students as both lecturer and discipline coordinator for the course. His *Sampler* essay explores how his transition from researcher in the basic sciences to that of educator in medicine has broadened and enriched both endeavors.

Bradley Tober is an assistant professor of graphic design in the School of Art and Design. His research explores the potential of emerging code-based and interactive visual communication technologies, with the objective of developing (often speculative) applications of them to design practice and pedagogy. He is particularly interested in examining the designer's role as a mediator between technologies and their users. His contribution to the *Sampler* discusses how his roles as design practitioner/industry professional, researcher, and educator coincide to foster student engagement with the intersections of design and technology.

Agniezska Tuszynska, who received her doctorate in American literature in May 2013, taught a literature class for the Education Justice Project, and currently is an assistant professor at Queensborough Community College (CUNY).

Bryan Wilcox is an iFoundry postdoctoral fellow and interdisciplinary senior design course coordinator. He has held engineering positions at General Electric, Northrup Grumman, and John Deere. Bryan also cofounded the Product Manufactory. He is the instructor of the IEFX Projects course.

Kate Williams is an assistant professor in the Graduate School of Library and Information Science. Her research focuses on community informatics, which is the study of how local communities use information technology (IT). This has included studying IT use by Champaign Urbana's nonprofit and government agencies during the local area broadband installation, as well as learning about digital divides and public libraries in Beijing. Her work prioritizes social capital and local agency in the information revolution. For the *Sampler*, she explains how she implements the university's land-grant mission by rooting her teaching in service and research, both on campus and in her school's award-winning distance program.

Mary-Ann Winkelmes is coordinator of instructional development and research at the University of Nevada, Las Vegas, where she is also an affiliate scholar in the Department of History. At the University of Illinois, she founded the Transparency in Learning and Teaching in Higher Education project, for which she received the POD Network's Robert J. Menges Award for Outstanding Research in Educational Development. She has published on learning and teaching in higher education, and on the history of art and architecture in Renaissance Italy, Benedictine church design and decoration, acoustics, and religious architecture.

The University of Illinois Press
is a founding member of the
Association of American University Presses.

Composed in 10/13 Sabon LT Std
by Celia Shapland
at the University of Illinois Press
Manufactured by Sheridan Books, Inc.

University of Illinois Press
1325 South Oak Street
Champaign, IL 61820-6903
www.press.uillinois.edu